The Ferrari
Dino 246, 308 and 328

The Ferrari
Dino 246, 308 and 328

A collector's guide
by Alan Henry

MOTOR RACING PUBLICATIONS LTD
Unit 6, The Pilton Estate, 46 Pitlake, Croydon CR0 3RY, England

ISBN 0 947981 23 3
First published 1988

Copyright © 1988 Alan Henry and Motor Racing Publications Ltd

All rights reserved. No part of this publication may be reproduced, stored in a retrieval system, or transmitted, in any form or by any means, electronic, mechanical, photocopying, recording or otherwise, without the prior permission of Motor Racing Publications Ltd

Photoset and printed in Great Britain by
Netherwood, Dalton & Co Ltd
Bradley Mills, Huddersfield, West Yorkshire

Contents

Introduction			6
Acknowledgements			8
Chapter 1	Setting the scene	At the sign of the Prancing Horse	9
Chapter 2	In memory of Dino	Prototypes and the 206GT	13
Chapter 3	Dino 246GT and GTS	Ferraris by another name	21
Chapter 4	On track	Racing Dino 166P, 206S and F2	31
Chapter 5	308GT4	V8 engine and 2 + 2 Bertone body	36
Chapter 6	308GTB and GTS	Beautiful classics	47
Chapter 7	Mondial 8	Fuel injection introduced	61
Chapter 8	308 Quattrovalvole and 328	Regaining the edge	71
Chapter 9	What to look for	Buying and running a small Ferrari	87
Chapter 10	288GTO and F40	Blood brothers	97
Chapter 11	The Fiat Dinos	Second cousins	108
Chapter 12	The wider family	Dino-engined Lancias	113
Chapter 13	Made in Maranello	What goes into a Ferrari	119
Appendix A	Technical specifications		125
Appendix B	Production figures and chassis numbers including UK market allocations		127
Appendix C	Performance figures		128

Introduction

The Ferraris dealt with in this volume are perhaps the most significant ever built by what is regarded by its fans as the most exclusive car maker in the world. At face value, those words may seem a trifle weighty, bearing in mind that, although we touch on the 288GTO and the F40, the main thrust of the book deals with the 'volume' end of the Ferrari range over the past two decades. But that, of course, is why they are such significant machines.

As I write these words, Ferrari is a booming prestige division of the Fiat empire which is allowed sufficient autonomy to retain its own idiosyncracies within an effective overall business administration. Yet it is less than 20 years since Enzo Ferrari, his company suffering worrying cash-flow problems, his road car sales producing insufficient income for him to sustain his racing programmes at the sort of level he had become accustomed to, sought to shelter beneath the protective financial umbrella proffered by Gianni Agnelli.

This, then, is the story of the road cars which helped Ferrari march back to economic health in the 1970s and 1980s, the cars which enabled the company to become truly profitable and economically sound. From the jewel-like Dino 246, with its cammy, race-bred V6, through to the flexible refinement of the current 328GTB and Mondial models, which now offer customers a level of refinement, build quality and mechanical dependability which would have seemed impossible to envisage at the start of the story.

Ferraris can be glorious, yet infuriating machines. I have struggled out of London in rush-hour traffic in a series of GTBs and Mondials over the last decade, convinced that I never wanted to see, drive or sit in another one. Yet, within 24 hours, on the empty, rolling, open country roads in North Essex and Suffolk, those frustrating memories quickly faded and, repeatedly, I fell under the spell of the Prancing Horse. I defy any truly enthusiastic road driver to say he does not feel the same way.

Tillingham, Essex
April, 1988

ALAN HENRY

Acknowledgements

Several people have helped and guided me with this project, so my thanks are due to Ken Bradshaw, of the Ferrari Owners' Club; Shaun Bealey and Mark Konig, at Maranello Concessionaries; Terry Hoyle; Daryll Group and David Hunt. The publishers, MRP, have remained supremely patient and long-suffering as deadlines came and went and I am grateful to editor Ray Hutton for contributing Chapter 13.

Apart from my own efforts with a camera, the photographic content of this book has come from a number of sources, and in particular I would like to record my thanks to Neill Bruce, *Classic and Sportscar* magazine, Ray Hutton, Motor News and Features and Patrick Stephenson, who between them managed to fill a number of important gaps in the picture coverage.

A.H.

Setting the scene

At the sign of the Prancing Horse

From the moment the first car bearing the Ferrari name saw the light of day in 1947, Enzo Ferrari's passion has been overwhelmingly for his racing cars. It is probably a bit extreme to suggest that his road car manufacturing operation was a 'necessary evil' providing commercial underpinning for his lavish Grand Prix and sports car programmes, but that is the way many people at Maranello regarded it in the 1950s and early 1960s.

Sustaining the reputation of the Prancing Horse as a dominant, secure force on the race tracks of the world was a number-one priority. Road cars, invariably on the primitive side as far as handling and braking were concerned, had their hearts in a series of superb 12-cylinder engines and were clothed in elegant custom-built bodies produced by some of the world's most prestigious coachbuilders.

Ferrari road cars had a breathtakingly exclusive cachet in those early years, purchased as they were in tiny numbers by royalty, international playboys, film stars and the glitterati of 'cafe society' – the forerunners of what we might now describe as the jet set. The likelihood of one of these automotive jewels being owned by, say, a Chipping Norton builder, was, to put it mildly, rather small!

Then Fiat came along and changed all that, helping Ferrari to popularize his marque in a manner that would have seemed impossible in those pioneering days of the early 1950s. It was not a sudden process, for the subtle influence of Italy's major car maker had helped Ferrari behind the scenes for many years before control of the company passed into Fiat's hands after a

momentous meeting between Gianni Agnelli and Enzo Ferrari in the summer of 1969.

Enzo Ferrari's life was first touched by Fiat many decades earlier. His first contact with them had been within weeks of the end of the First World War when, in dire need of a job during the winter of 1918/19, he turned up at Fiat's Turin headquarters with a letter of introduction from the Colonel of his army regiment.

He was received courteously enough by Ing. Diego Soria, but it was explained to the young Ferrari that Fiat was not sufficiently large an operation to provide jobs for all the ex-servicemen who had been knocking on their front door.

At only 21 years of age, the young Ferrari was already a fervent admirer of Fiat and, in particular, of the dynamic leadership of Senator Giovanni Agnelli (grandfather of the current head of the Agnelli dynasty), and was understandably disappointed to be turned down. He walked away from the factory little realizing how many times he would be talking to Fiat people over the next 50 years – or in what role.

His next contact with Fiat came in the role of 'raider' of the very engineering department of which he had so dearly hoped to become a part. His great passion was motor racing, and by 1920 he had joined Alfa Romeo, for whom he was to drive with distinction between intermittent bouts of ill-health. However, it was Ferrari's talent for organization and administration which most impressed his employers, and soon he was enticing some of Fiat's top racing engineers away from Turin to Milan as he built up Alfa's racing department. During this period his reputation

Enzo Ferrari, who always looked upon his production cars as a means of financing his racing activities, relinquished control of their manufacture to Fiat in 1969, two years after the introduction of the Dino 206GT.

within the sport grew impressively, not least amongst his contemporaries at Fiat, whose own racing programme had been scaled down considerably.

This marked the start of the Ferrari legend. When Alfa Romeo in turn decided to cut back on their racing in the late 1920s, the stage was set for the formation of Scuderia Ferrari, an independent racing preparation and management organization which Enzo Ferrari established in premises in Modena, to co-ordinate the racing activities of wealthy amateur drivers and, eventually, to run what was effectively a quasi-works Alfa Romeo team.

The Scuderia's emblem was the shield bearing a prancing horse which had been presented to Ferrari in 1923 on the occasion of his victory in the Circuit of Ravenna. It was donated by the parents of Italian fighter pilot Francesco Baracca, who had been killed shortly before the end of the war.

Of course, by the late 1930s, another World War was looming on the horizon, and in Fascist Italy, under the heel of dictator Mussolini, independent enterprise sat uncomfortably alongside the political doctrine of collective material achievement. The Scuderia Ferrari had enjoyed many successes since 1930, but Alfa Romeo were 'advised' to take their racing activities back in-house. When Alfa Corsa was formed in 1938, they also took back Enzo Ferrari to manage it. At this point, his Scuderia, in which Alfa Romeo had only recently acquired a majority interest, was liquidated.

By then, however, Enzo Ferrari was so used to running his own show that becoming an employee again was something he found intolerable. Within a few months there was another parting of the ways and Ferrari established Auto Avio Construzioni at the former Scuderia Ferrari premises, from which he built a couple of 1½-litre, straight-eight-cylinder sports cars for the 1940 Mille Miglia. Under the terms of his Alfa Romeo contract he was not permitted to lend his name to any rival car for at least four years after leaving the company, so the cars were known simply as Tipo 815s. In all but name they were the first Ferraris.

For much of the Second World War, Ferrari ran a machine tool business, first from his Modena premises and later in less cramped surroundings, at nearby Maranello, where he already owned some land. The Maranello factory was quite badly damaged late in the war, but then rebuilt and enlarged by 1946, and then the following year the first car to bear the Ferrari name, the 125C (a two-seater sports car fitted with a 1½-litre V12 engine driving through a five-speed gearbox) was given its competition debut on May 11 at Piacenza.

While established car manufacturers concerned themselves with the task of producing some cars for sale to the public, leaving thought of competition involvement to a later day, Enzo Ferrari was determined to pursue what was financially a much more precarious policy. First and foremost he was a racer, so he would build cars to be raced, either by the factory or by those customers who could afford to both buy and race them. He would also build cars for the road, but these would be derived from his competition cars and the revenue from them would be used to help finance his competition activities.

Ferrari's total output in the first six years barely touched 130 cars. But 1953 saw an agreement reached with Pininfarina for the series-production of the 212 model, followed the next year by the first of the 250GTs, variations of which would last through to the early 1960s.

Enzo Ferrari had always hoped that his son Dino, born in 1932, would grow up to assume control of the company. But Dino never enjoyed robust health and, although he studied single-mindedly to take an engineering degree in Switzerland, determined to earn himself a firm technical understanding of the details of automotive engineering, Enzo Ferrari became increasingly concerned for his son's well-being during the early 1950s.

The truth was that Dino Ferrari suffered from muscular dystrophy, and he was fighting a losing battle against the cruelly debilitating disease. Despite his deteriorating health, he assisted his father and former Lancia V8 Formula 1 designer Vittorio Jano in the task of preparing an engine for the new 1½-litre Formula 2 which was scheduled to start in 1957.

In his tortured memoirs, Enzo Ferrari gives Dino credit for finalizing the V6 layout which was to give rise to one of the most famous engines in the marque's racing history. We must allow Ferrari Senior some emotional latitude when it comes to assessing the validity of his claim, for Dino died of nephritis, a kidney disease, on June 30, 1956, a tragic loss from which Enzo Ferrari has never recovered.

Dino's name would be perpetuated on some of the most exciting and historically significant road and racing cars manufactured by Ferrari over the next 20 years, including, of course, a car which really starts the main thrust of this volume, that delectable little jewel, the Dino 246...

There was a less obvious aspect to consider in the wake of Dino Ferrari's death. His father was already 58 years old and apparently without an heir (his illegitimate son Piero Lardi was not formally acknowledged as a blood relative until the early 1980s, after the death of Ferrari's wife Laura) and it was becoming increasingly clear to him that an association with a major volume manufacturer would be the only sensible route to follow.

Ford made a pitch for the business in the early 1960s. Ferrari initially agreed to a take-over, then had second thoughts and, confronted by hordes of sharply-dressed Detroit executives, threw up his hands in horror and aborted the deal. Periodically

The Dino name, adopted in memory of Ferrari's son who died in 1956, was first seen on the cam covers of racing engines. Here is Tony Brooks preparing for the 1959 Aintree 200 in his Dino 246-powered single-seater. He finished second behind Jean Behra's Dino 256.

Peter Collins on his way to victory in the 1958 British Grand Prix at Silverstone at the wheel of his Ferrari Dino 246. Tragically, this talented and popular driver was to be killed two weeks later during the German Grand Prix at the Nurburgring.

during the 1960s rumours would spread round the motoring world linking Ferrari to one of the major multi-national car companies, but, in the back of most people's minds, there was only one really appropriate suitor: Fiat. By the late 1960s Ferrari was hard-pressed to make financial ends meet, so on June 18, 1969, he journeyed to Fiat's Turin headquarters and struck a deal with Gianni Agnelli, the debonair and highly regarded 49-year-old who controlled the Fiat Group.

The new partnership saw Fiat take a half share in Ferrari SpA's stock and take over its road car manufacturing operation. The racing division remained totally under Enzo Ferrari's control. The arrangement with Fiat was concluded *in vitalizio*, which means that Fiat effectively paid Ferrari an annuity for the balance of his life for the privilege of using his property and facilities. On Enzo Ferrari's death the whole manufacturing facility is ceded to Fiat. They have been paying for almost 20 years.

There was no sudden change to be seen in Ferrari's *modus operandi* the following day, for Fiat not only knew precisely what it had acquired, but Agnelli appreciated exactly what sort of benefits could be drawn from the partnership. Fiat was now actively and closely associated with one of the most romantic and prestigious names in the car world. In most people's eyes, Ferrari represented Italian technical and engineering prestige at its best. When Ferrari raced, it was *Italy* that raced. For Fiat, the rub-off would be tremendous; it would enhance their image in the world. For Ferrari, it was a financial life-line which would ensure the continuity of the marque as a low-volume specialist car maker.

The golden era of Ferrari road cars was just beginning.

CHAPTER 2

In memory of Dino

Prototypes and the 206GT

The first Dino engine appeared in 1957, a 65-degrees V6 used in the works Ferrari Formula 2 single-seaters. Developed from the design discussions between Jano, Ferrari and his son, the 1,489cc engine had first burst into life on the test bed five months after Dino's death.

It was originally to have been a 60-degrees V6, the additional 5 degrees being added to accommodate twin overhead camshafts for each bank of cylinders. The first Dino was a classic engine which, revised and revamped in many different configurations, sustained Ferrari's Formula 1 challenge through into the following decade.

This is not, however, the Dino V6 which starts this story and led to the expansion of the Ferrari road car line. The origins of that are some seven years later. In December 1964, Enzo Ferrari held a press conference at the Hotel Real-Fini in Modena to outline the Scuderia's competition plans for the 1965 season. Almost as an afterthought, Mr Ferrari mentioned a new Dino 168 GT car.

The designation suggested a 1.6-litre eight-cylinder engine. Though the Ferrari Formula 1 cars of the time had eight cylinders, this created confusion among the audience, which Mr Ferrari was not prepared to clarify. Though it would have to be restricted to six cylinders, a 1.6-litre engine made sense as the basis of a racing power unit for the new 1.6-litre Formula 2, which was due to start in 1967.

Though his main interest was in the top echelons of racing – Formula 1 and the classic sports car endurance races – Ferrari felt under some pressure to compete in Formula 2. He wanted a 'stepping stone' for Italian drivers. But the new rules were not in

his favour. To encourage the bigger manufacturers and keep costs down, they called for 'production-based' engines, derived from road cars of which at least 500 a year were produced. At that time, the Ferrari factory was making about 700 cars a year; clearly they could not nearly double production simply to go Formula 2 racing.

The solution rested with Fiat. The go-between was Francesco Bellicardi, general manager of the Weber carburettor firm, owned by Fiat and a long-time supplier to Ferrari. It was he who brought Ferrari's F2 engine problem to the attention of Gianni Agnelli. The upshot was that Fiat agreed to build a run of Ferrari-designed engines and to offer them in a low-volume series of Fiat sports cars, as well as supplying them for Ferrari road cars.

This, then, can be seen as a very significant point in Ferrari history. It linked Ferrari and Fiat more closely than ever before. It produced a 'baby' Ferrari that would lead to a complete change in Ferrari's road car production and it led to a series of Fiats that reflected in the glory of Italy's world-famous racing team. Ironically, the Formula 2 cars that were its *raison d'être* were to prove the least successful aspect of the project.

It was not the first time that Ferrari had considered some kind of co-operation to produce road cars in larger volumes than the exotic V12s and the Maranello facilities would allow. In 1959, they had produced an experimental four-cylinder engine of just 849cc, producing some 75bhp. It was installed into a squarish Pininfarina coupe body. This 'Ferrarina' was the object of discussion between Ferrari and a number of potential manufacturers. It came to nothing, but a development of the idea, with a

Like so many exotic cars, the Dino 206 began life as a show car, Pininfarina presenting this Dino Berlinetta Speciale at the 1965 Paris Salon. The four-headlamp frontal treatment was the subject of one of several major revisions to be made before the car could be considered a practical production model.

The low roof of the show prototype was another impractical feature, but the sweeping buttresses flanking the engine cover would form an attractive feature of the final design. This car, which was built on a sports-racing chassis, had its 2-litre 206P engine mounted longitudinally.

Designated the Dino Berlinetta GT and much closer to the final design, this second prototype appeared at the 1966 Turin Show. The smooth nose, flanked by wing-mounted headlamps, and the five-spoke alloy wheels (still secured by three-eared spinners) were to be adopted for the production Dino, but there was still some work to be done on the roof-to-tail line.

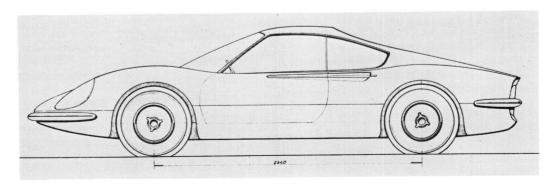

95bhp 1,032cc version of the engine and a beautiful little fastback GT body by Bertone, became the ASA Mille and enjoyed a short production run in 1964/65.

In 1964, a prototype was produced for Innocenti, the Milan manufacturer which at that time built BMC cars under licence. It was, in effect, the precursor of the Fiat Dino – a front-engined 2 + 2 coupe with a Bertone body and a Ferrari engine. This, intriguingly, was to be a single-cam 1.8-litre version of the original Dino V6. Innocenti decided not to proceed to production.

Though Enzo Ferrari's tantalizing announcement at the end of 1964 had suggested an eight-cylinder, the Dino that did make it to the market place turned out to be another V6. It was developed by Franco Rocchi, later to design Ferrari Formula 1 engines. Like the earlier Dino, its cylinders were disposed at 65 degrees to allow four overhead camshafts, driven by primary reduction gears and chains.

First appearance for this engine was in the sleek little Dino 166P racers entered in the Monza 1000Kms sports car race. (Their story is covered in chapter 4.) The first road car application shown to the public was the Dino Berlinetta Speciale exhibited by Pininfarina at the 1965 Paris Salon. Though not a runner, this was built on a sports-racing chassis and had a 1,986cc engine, as used by the competition department in the 206P which won the 1965 European Mountain Championship.

Pininfarina's show car was the shape of things to come. Like the racing Dinos, it had its engine amidships, mounted longitudinally with the gearbox behind the rear axle line. Though the first mid-engined Ferrari racing car had appeared as long before as 1960 and the 250LM sports-racer was built in a small series as a 'homologation special', the Dino Speciale showed that Ferrari's new baby would be their first purpose-built road car with its engine behind the driver. To a company whose production cars had always shown a close relationship to their racing machines this was an important move.

The Paris show car had a very low roof-line and four headlights snuggling beneath a full-width Plexiglass cover in the car's nose. It featured 10-hole alloy wheels with triple-eared 'spinners' reminiscent of the Ferrari 330P2 endurance racer and the 330GTC road car. Though unquestionably a striking piece of machinery, it did not have the classically balanced lines which

would eventually make the Dino 206 – and the 246 – such a delightful confection.

The second prototype was the Dino Berlinetta GT, first shown at the Turin Show in November 1966. This turned out to be far closer to the final design than the earlier machine. With a higher roof-line giving the whole package a much better proportioned air, this offering had its headlights faired into the front wings behind covers and sported more elegant 'five star' Campagnolo alloy wheels. Like the Speciale, its engine was mounted in-line. It was set against the scene of the Fiat Dino's release, the latter being offered in either two-door spider or coupe form – at prices considerably lower than those anticipated for the Ferrari version of the Dino.

At the 1967 Frankfurt Show, enthusiasts savoured yet another Pininfarina styling exercise, the Dino Berlinetta Competizione which had more in common with the 206P than the Berlinetta GT, although it was still a closed car. Gull-wing doors were fitted behind a huge, double-curvature windscreen, and it sported outlandish adjustable front and rear wings, large extractor louvres ahead of the screen and similar ones behind covers in the rear wings.

The definitive Dino finally emerged at the Turin Show later in 1967. In appearance, the 206GT was very close to the Berlinetta GT of the previous year, but under the skin there was a fundamental difference: the engine was mounted transversely, and accompanied by a completely new transmission mounted parallel to the engine and sharing its sump casting (though lubrication of gearbox and differential was kept separate from the engine). This was the logical power-train layout for a mid-engined road car as it allowed a reasonable luggage compartment behind the engine.

Even then, after two years of teasing with show cars, Ferrari were not ready to start production, and it would be well into 1968 before the 206GT became available to the first customers. When it did, there was no Ferrari nameplate or Prancing Horse badge to be seen; the management at Maranello insisted the Dino should be a totally separate 'range within a range'.

The production version of the Dino 206GT was a gem; its superbly-rounded bodywork was styled by Pininfarina and manufactured in alloy by Scaglietti. A composite platform chassis structure of elliptical-section welded steel tubes supported

There was a strong family resemblance between Pininfarina's Dino and the Ferrari 365P Berlinetta Speciale show car which also appeared in Turin in 1966. This radical design featured three-across seating with a central driving position, just ahead of the two passenger seats, with the gear lever to the driver's right.

the bodywork. Independent suspension was employed all round, utilizing unequal-length pressed-steel double wishbones with outboard-mounted coil spring/damper units front and rear, and an anti-roll bar at the front. The Dino 206 broke new ground by being the first 'Ferrari' to be equipped with rack-and-pinion steering.

The all-alloy 1,986cc (86 × 57mm) 65-degree V6 was more highly tuned than the version already used in the Fiat Dino coupe and spider, developing 180bhp at 8,000rpm with a 9.2:1 compression ratio and three Weber 40DCN twin-choke carburettors. Made in Turin, the engines were installed at Maranello. The twin overhead camshafts on each bank were chain-driven, the valves themselves actuated directly by bucket tappets. Power was transmitted by a diaphragm-spring clutch to the primary shaft of the all-synchromesh five-speed gearbox by means of three pinions, thence via two spur gears through the differentials to the drive-shafts, which were, of course, parallel to the crankshaft of the transverse-mounted V6 engine.

Although the production Dino was soon to be announced, Pininfarina could not resist a spot more fun on the show car theme. This time it was the Dino Prototipo Competizione, a car which borrowed more from the racing Dinos than from the forthcoming road car. Gullwing doors, angled dual headlamps, large front and rear extractor vents and adjustable wings combined to give the car a purposeful but far from elegant appearance.

The Dino 206 in its production form. Compared with the second prototype the front quarter bumpers and the grille opening have been deepened a little and the five-spoke wheels have given way to a Cromodora design incorporating six ventilation slots and pairs of stiffening ribs.

Apart from being slightly shorter overall than the soon-to-follow Dino 246GT, tell-tale signs by which the 206GT can be identified include the 14in Cromodora six-hole cast-alloy wheels with triple-eared 'spinners', on which were mounted 185 × 14in radial-ply tyres, and the chromed fuel filler cap just behind the nearside rear side window.

The single most striking aspect of the whole styling package was adjudged the concave rear screen hidden between the long 'buttresses', which swept rearwards and downwards from the roof-line into the rear wings.

The water radiator was mounted in the nose of the car with a thermostatically-controlled electric fan. As the spare wheel accounted for all the remaining space under the 'bonnet', room for luggage was confined to the carpeted compartments immediately behind the engine. You could just about squeeze a briefcase behind the reclined-position driving seat.

Two views which expose the classic elegance of Pininfarina's definitive Dino 206GT. Approximately 150 examples were to be built, all of them with left-hand drive, before the car was upgraded into the 246GT in 1969.

Instrumentation was to a high standard (described in detail in connection with the 246) and electrically-operated side windows were offered as options, although these were standard equipment on the cars sold in the UK.

There were not many of those. Ferrari factory records show that only 152 206GTs were made in the 18 months or so it was in production. Just five of these came to the UK via the official importers Maranello Concessionaries. All were left-hand drive; the factory did not produce this model with right-hand drive.

The Dino 206 was heaped with praise by everyone who drove it. Britain's *Car* magazine was typically eulogistic: 'Driving the Dino is quite an experience, for it is probably closer to a mid-engined racing car than to most road vehicles'.

Performance, though good by the standards of the time, was not, however, of the racing car kind: 0-60mph in 7.6sec, standing quarter-mile in just under 16sec and a maximum of 140mph. The Dino's main competitor, the Porsche 911S, was quicker, and by August 1969 it had a bigger engine – 2.2 litres, up from 2 litres.

Something had to be done, and the result was the Dino 246GT.

CHAPTER 3

Dino 246GT and GTS

Ferraris by another name

The Dino 246GT, unveiled at the Geneva Motor Show in spring 1969, arrived at a key time for Ferrari. It would not be ready for production for some months (after delays, they had been building the 206GT for less than a year), by which time Ferrari's *riparto industriale* would be under Fiat control.

Ferrari already knew what they had to do. The Dino needed more power to match the performance of Porsche and the increasing competition from other 'mini-supercars'. The Maranello factory and the associated Scaglietti body works in Modena had to be geared up to the demands of larger-scale production. Not mass-production, of course, but aiming perhaps to double their annual record of 740 cars established in 1965.

The first objective was tackled by adopting a 2.4-litre version of the V6 engine using a cast-iron block, a departure from Ferrari's normal practice (adopted for the 206) of an alloy block with shrunken-in steel cylinder liners.

Scaglietti had to equip itself with more substantial tooling and would then be able to make the Dino bodies in steel. While a change from light alloy to steel made sense from the point-of-view of speed and production consistency, and meant that the bodies were less prone to damage from careless hands, it was guaranteed to turn all but the most fastidiously maintained 246s into 'rust buckets' within a decade!

Fiat's management hastened Ferrari's progressive plans and also put in hand a considerable enlargement of the Maranello factory – adding 100,000sq ft to the 170,000sq ft at the time of the take-over. This would be finished towards the end of 1970 and it was not until then that Dino 246 production could really get into top gear.

Though, at a glance, virtually identical to the first production Dino, the 246GT had a 2.3in longer wheelbase and was 3.7in longer overall.

The new engine – also used for new versions of the Fiat Dino – had bore and stroke dimensions of 92.5 × 60mm, making 2,419cc. Like its predecessor, the crankshaft was supported by four main bearings and the light-alloy cylinder heads had double overhead camshafts driven by chains.

In its Ferrari application, with triple Weber 40DCF carburettors, it produced 195bhp (DIN) at 7,600rpm, an increase of 15bhp over the 2-litre car with considerably better torque spread (166lb/ft (DIN) at 5,500rpm as opposed to 138lb/ft at 6,500rpm on the 206).

The bigger engine sliced 1.2sec off its 0-60mph best and would top 148mph in ideal conditions. Yet frustratingly, it was still not quite quick enough. It measured up well up against the 2.2-litre Porsche 911S, but then a 2.4-litre version of the German machine was made available...

There was no question of Ferrari getting away from making a right-hand-drive model if the UK market potential for the new car was to be fully tapped, but this necessitated a completely different chassis frame to that employed on the all-LHD 206 range. Maranello Concessionaries were absolutely insistent that the factory should offer RHD, but the north/south central chassis member on the 206 was slightly off-set to the right, making it impossible to transfer the pedal box to that side of the car. This was duly altered on the 246 chassis.

The UK price for the 246 was far more competitive than it had been for the 2-litre car. Maranello Concessionaries' then-

A popular way of identifying a 246GT from a 206GT is to look at the wheels. Those of the larger-engined car are normally secured by five studs instead of a central spinner.

This is a 1971 Dino, virtually unchanged, although the door lock has been repositioned slightly higher and now nestles in the cutaway section ahead of the rear air intake.

A batch of Dino 246 engines awaiting installation alongside the assembly line at Maranello. This and the photograph below were taken by Neill Bruce during a visit to the Ferrari factory in May 1973.

Just like Enzo Ferrari himself, his employees are never happier than when working with one of his jewel-like engines. This inverted V6 reveals the substantial ribbing on the sides and base of the sump.

managing director Shaun Bealey well recalls that 'the LHD Dino 206 was priced at £6,250, so customers for it were justifiably a bit miffed when the right-hand-drive version of the 246 came on to the market a year later at something around £1,000 less!'. In fact, by the time the first Dino 246 arrived in the UK in October 1970 it was priced at £5,485 63p. The car was well accepted on the British market, where 488 of the 246GT's 2,487 total production run were sold, while the later detachable-roof 246GTS sold 235 out of its 1,274 total in the UK.

It was in the spring of 1971 that I first became acquainted with the Dino 246GT. My friend Brian Hart, whose race engine preparation company is now part of Cosworth Engineering, decided to break away from his staple diet of 3-litre Ford Capris and treat himself to a Dino 246GT. Tucked tight into the passenger seat, looking out through that curvaceous windscreen across those evocatively shaped front wings, I recall him winging me through the Essex lanes with that rasping V6 echoing its shrill, high-revving message from a few inches behind our heads. And he made a comment that has stuck in my mind for the best part of two decades: 'It feels just like a road-going Formula 2

Dino body assembly took place at the Scaglietti factory, from where bodies were transported to Maranello for final assembly and finishing. The slot for the repeater light behind the headlamp identifies the car in the foreground as one destined for the US market, while the car behind it has extended wing flares to accept wider tyres.

Brabham BT30 with slightly softer springs!'. Brian was well qualified to know what he was talking about for, at the time, he was still driving the occasional race for Bob Gerard's private team – in a Brabham BT30.

Inside the 246GT cockpit there is hardly sufficient surplus room to accommodate a toothbrush, although Ferrari had happily avoided producing a typically Italian driving position suitable for only those with short legs and longer than average arms. The leather-trimmed seats offer little more than basic support – most commentators judge them far too narrow – but the fore/aft adjustment is more than adequate to cater for a 6ft 2in frame without too much trouble. The three-spoke leather-trimmed steering wheel and typical steel-gated gearchange for the five-speed 'box fall snugly to hand and can be reached easily with the driver wearing seat belts. The pedals are slightly off-set to the left.

The 246's elliptical instrument panel provides a speedometer on the left, incorporating trip and total milometers, with a matching rev-counter positioned on the right. In between these two major gauges are oil temperature and oil pressure gauges, plus water temperature and fuel contents gauges (the 14½-Imperial gallon petrol tank is a gallon larger than that on the 206).

At each outer extremity of the ellipse, shrouded neatly by the driver's hands at the '10-to-2' position, are the ammeter (left) and clock (right).

Two stalks protrude from the steering column on the left-hand side, a single one on the right. The inner one on the left controls the direction indicators, while the twisting motion of the outer stalk deals with sidelights/headlights/main beam headlights. The right-hand stalk controls the windscreen washers and wipers, the latter having no intermittent mode, merely a rheostat-controlled variable speed facility. The wipers sweep outwards from the centre of the screen, covering a wide arc into its outer corners, but tall drivers complain of a 'missed area' at the top in the centre of the screen.

As far as accessibility for servicing purposes is concerned, the transverse engine installation in the Dino 246 unquestionably poses problems. Small details highlight the point: for example, the oil dipstick is difficult to thread into its tube in the forward-facing bank of cylinders. Moreover, there is no access panel in the bulkhead behind the passenger compartment, so even rectifying relatively minor defects such as a blown cylinder head gasket could end up a long (and consequently expensive) undertaking. Removing the engine and transmission package is facilitated by a removable panel at the rear of the boot and detachable panels within the wheelarches.

It was not until spring 1972 that the Dino 246 found its way on to the US market where, predictably, it was received with considerable acclaim. The respected *Road & Track* summed its appeal up by saying: 'Ferrari name or no, the Dino is a Ferrari

Closer to the end of the Scaglietti assembly line, a 246GTS followed by a 246GT have already accumulated much of their electrical equipment.

For many years synonymous with Ferraris on the track, Michael Salmon takes a turn at the wheel of Maranello Concessionaires' right-hand drive demonstration car FPA 132J in March 1971.

and the mystique plus the exciting shape plus the sounds plus the great chassis all adds up to a lot of car'. But they added the rider that the Dino did not really shape up against the Porsche 911S in terms of straight-line performance, neither did it compare with its corresponding German rival on price. In the spring of 1972, the US price was $14,500 (East Coast) and $13,885 (West Coast). By comparison, the 911S came in at $9,249 for the five-speed gearbox model. It was also considerably lighter; even the relatively heavy Targa version of the 911 weighed 300lb less than the Dino coupe.

Of course, from the performance standpoint, the Dino 246 had to be 'federalized', and it was no straightforward task to make the modifications necessary for it to conform with the US safety and pollution control regulations. Ferrari engineers experimented with fuel injection as a possible alternative to the three Weber carburettors, but they eventually opted for a system similar to that employed on their 12-cylinder cars; an air injection pump which was designed to supply fresh air to the exhaust ports, combined with an electromagnetic clutch that disengaged the pump at engine speeds above 3,500rpm, thereby minimizing power loss at higher revs. These modifications accounted for some of the additional weight carried by the US-market cars and also cut peak power by about 10% (down 20bhp to a quoted 175bhp at 7,000rpm). The 0-60mph time for the 'federal' car increased to 7.9sec, which was slower than the original Dino 206.

No doubt with an eye to greater sales in the US, Ferrari commissioned Pininfarina to draw up an open-topped version of the Dino. The result, the 246GTS, did not appear until quite late

Identified by Pininfarina as a 1969 246GT, this Dino has the three-eared central wheel nuts normally associated with the earlier 206GT. Note also that the coachbuilder's corporate badge has been added above their nameplate just behind the door.

The pleasurable working environment of a Dino driver. The ammeter and clock may be partly hidden by the steering wheel rim, but the oil and water temperature, oil pressure and fuel gauges are prominently on show between the rev-counter and speedometer. The heater and fresh air controls are above the radio and there are three steering column stalks.

When they were new, Dinos were strictly Dinos, not Ferraris, but this owner is proud of his car's heritage, witness the Prancing Horse and Ferrari badges as well as the Dino GT plate. Pity about the left rear bumper, though!

The 246GTS with its removable top was a logical extension to the Dino range and became an instant success following its debut at the 1972 Geneva Show. Inevitably, three-quarter rear vision is more restricted than in the coupe, but spider owners are more than content to put up with the inconvenience to judge by the popularity of this model.

This view of a 246GTS, kindly supplied from the archives of *Classic and Sportscar* magazine, accentuates the smoothness of the car's body contours. This has to be one of the outstanding styling achievements of the 1960s.

Running changes to the 246 series during its production life included the upholstery, the seats in this instance incorporating transverse pleating extending all the way from the front of the cushions to the top of the backrests. Earlier cars had plain bolsters at each end of the seats.

in the model's five-year run. It was launched at the 1972 Geneva Show. Not strictly a convertible, but rather a 'targa' with a removable centre roof panel, the GTS became a very popular variant – 1,180 were made compared with 2,732 GTs over a much longer period – and this version is today the most covetable of all Dinos.

To compensate for the loss of roof strength, the GTS has a roll-hoop at the B-pillar and bodywork faired into the buttresses instead of rear quarter windows. The concave rear window remains fixed, as on the GT, and the roof panel stows away neatly behind the seats.

The 246GT and GTS continued in production side-by-side until May 1974. By then a successor – fixed roof only, but with 2+2 seating – had been revealed. It was still a Dino, but the proud lineage of the V6 was discontinued. The 308GT4 had a new V8.

CHAPTER 4

On track

Racing Dino 166P, 206S and F2

Although the 206/246 were pivotally important cars in the marque's contemporary history, no account of their role would be complete without mention of the competition cars that were predicted by that announcement at Ferrari's December 1964 press conference in Modena.

The first of the racing Dino 166Ps looked for all the world like a miniature 250LM, then one of Maranello's front-line racers, a private example of which would achieve Ferrari's last victory at Le Mans that same summer. Franco Rocchi's 65-degree V6 engine was derived from the Grand Prix power unit which had done such stalwart service over the previous five seasons. It had a bore and stroke of 77 × 57mm, producing a swept volume of 1,592cc. Using three twin-choke Weber 38DCN carburettors, the first racing Dino's power output was around 190bhp. It came to be regarded as a jewel of a car by those who used it in anger.

The 166P made its debut in the Monza 1000Kms in April 1965, when it was driven by Giancarlo Baghetti and Giampiero Biscaldi and qualified an impressive 12th only to blow up its engine after a few laps. The following month, the Dino scored its first victory at Vallelunga, near Rome, in Baghetti's hands, but the 'baby Ferrari' really put itself on the international racing map in the Nurburgring 1000Kms the following weekend where Lorenzo Bandini and Nino Vaccarella got it up to third overall behind two of the team's bigger V12-engined prototypes. Only a late pit stop to investigate a misfire (caused by a piece of rubber sealing material in the fuel system partially blocking a carburettor jet) ruined the symmetry of a Maranello 1-2-3 and allowed a Porsche into third place, the Dino resuming to take the chequered flag fourth overall.

After another engine failure at Le Mans, the 166P was handed to Ludovico Scarfiotti to contest the European Mountain Championship. This hillclimb series was an affair of considerable prestige and importance two decades ago, with Ferrari shaping up to serious factory opposition from both Porsche and Abarth. Scarfiotti may not have been a top-drawer Grand Prix driver, but he had developed into a notably talented hillclimb exponent.

For this exercise, the Dino was fitted with an experimental 86 × 57mm, 2-litre engine which developed just over 205bhp. Having missed the first two rounds of the series at Mont Ventoux and Rossfeld, Scarfiotti rattled off a succession of winning climbs at Trento-Bardone, Cesana-Sestrière, Freiburg, Ollon-Villars and Gaisberg to clinch the championship from Gerhard Mitter's Porsche.

For the 1966 racing season, it had been intended to produce 50 of these Dino 206s in order that the car could be homologated as a Group 4 2-litre sports car, but industrial problems prevented that and it had to continue running in the prototype class. Now clothed in brand new bodywork from Piero Drogo's factory in Modena, the engine was uprated to produce almost 220bhp and now, the 206S, as it became known, looked like a baby sister of the big 330P3, Maranello's main challenger for international sports car honours.

The highspot of the Dino's international season was when Bandini/Scarfiotti and the private North American Racing Team entry of Pedro Rodriguez/Richie Ginther finished second and third behind the Phil Hill/Jo Bonnier Chaparral in the Nurburgring 1000Kms. But on the hillclimb front, Scarfiotti lost his title to Porsche-mounted Mitter.

The factory kept racing the Dino 206S through into 1967, but it was a disaster. The works entries were generally entrusted to two young rising stars, Englishman Jonathan Williams and promising former Porsche driver Gunther Klass. The cars were plagued by endless reliability problems, seldom lasting through the endurance events for which they were entered, and the lowest point of the year came during practice at Mugello when Klass crashed into a tree and sustained fatal injuries. After that tragedy, the rather piecemeal participation in the European Mountain Championship came to an end and Porsche picked up those laurels for the second year running.

Allegedly, a total of 17 Dino 206SP racers were built, many of which enjoyed success in the hands of privateers across Europe during 1968 and 1969. The resourceful Alain de Cadenet was one such British-based *Ferrariste* who found his ex-Scuderia Brescia Corse 206S in a dilapidated condition in a field in northern Italy early in 1968. By his own admission, he didn't do too clever a deal over its purchase, but he returned it to the UK and successfully resuscitated it before crashing heavily at Crystal Palace in August the same year.

Dino engines came in many varieties, and in 1962 photographer Jeff Hutchinson spotted this rare Dino 286, a 60-degree V6 sports car power unit of 2,863cc (90 × 75mm) with a claimed power output of 260bhp at 6,800rpm.

This car started life as a Dino 166P coupe, initially with a 1.6-litre four-cam V6 engine, which was subsequently replaced by a 2-litre unit. In 1965 it reappeared with this open spider bodywork, in which form it was used by Ludovico Scarfiotti to win the European Mountain Championship — his second success in this contest.

This Dino 206S was entered in the name of Scuderia Nettuno for the 1967 Targa Florio, although it was effectively a works entry. The car was shared by Jonathan Williams and Vittorio Venturi, who finished fourth.

Ferrari slipped a 246 engine into this Dino spider for the 1967 Nurburgring 1000Kms race, but it broke during practice and Ludovico Scarfiotti and Günther Klass were left without a drive. So were Jean Guichet and Herbert Müller, whose 206S spider was burnt out following a practice accident. The previous year, 2-litre Dinos had finished second and third in this race behind the winning Chaparral.

Another view of the hybrid Dino 246P spider during practice at the Nurburgring. Here the car is tucked well in to the left going through the banked Karussel.

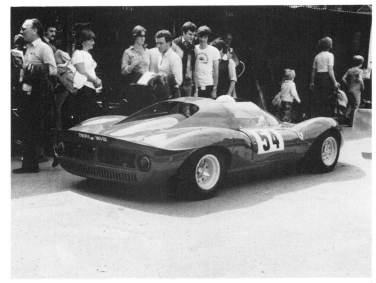

One of the first Dino 206S cars built, this is chassis number 004 and according to historian Doug Nye was originally one of the works cars and passed through several other hands before being restored by Dudley Mason-Styrron. Here the car is awaiting its turn at Shelsley Walsh hillclimb, where it was pictured by John Plummer.

De Cadenet swapped the wrecked car for a Porsche, but early the following year he acquired the ex-Tony Dean 206 which the Yorkshireman had used to great effect in national-level sports car events the previous summer. He enjoyed racing this baby Ferrari enormously, but eventually moved on to concentrate on competing in various Porsches during the early 1970s, his Dino being passed on to Anthony Bamford's collection and thence, in the case of the ex-Dean machine, to enthusiast Dudley Mason-Styrron.

It is appropriate to add a note about the racing career of the Formula 2 Ferrari which provided the inspiration for the Ferrari-Fiat Dino V6 engine. The Dino 166F2's 1.6-litre engine, derived from the all-alloy 2-litre and at first with three and later with four valves per cylinder, developed some 200bhp. It made its racing debut at Rouen, in 1967, driven by Jonathan Williams, but retired with engine failure and didn't appear again until the following season. Then, despite drivers of the class of Chris Amon and Jacky Ickx, results were slow to come, the cars being outclassed by the Ford Cosworth FVA-engined Brabhams and Matras.

A fine view of Mason-Styrron's Dino, this time at the Brighton Speed Trials. The Bentley driver alongside demonstrates just how far cockpit heights fell in four decades — almost as far as exhaust notes were raised!

The instrument which provides the music for the Dino 206S's exhaust pipes — the longitudinally mounted and fuel-injected V6 engine. Note the substantial trunking for cooling air on to the inboard brakes.

Towards the end of the 1968 season, not only did the Ferrari become a race winner, but the factory Formula 2 team began to achieve its objective of highlighting up-and-coming talent. Ernesto Brambilla scored the first win for the 166F2 at Hockenheim in October, with team-mate Derek Bell third, and Brambilla and Andrea De Adamich went on to take first and second places at Vallelunga. The year ended with a Formula 2 Temporada in Argentina, where the Ferraris won three out of four races so decisively that, in retrospect, several of their rivals wondered whether they used over-size engines! Certainly, the F2 cars were never as competitive again, though by using 2.4-litre versions of the Dino engine they had three years of success in the Tasman Series in Australia and New Zealand.

CHAPTER 5

308GT4

V8 engine and 2 + 2 Bertone body

Looking back, it is perhaps not surprising that the Dino 308GT4 was received by Ferrari enthusiasts with mixed feelings. The Dino 246 had not only become a classic in its own production span, but it had pioneered what, for want of a better word, we can refer to as the concept of the 'baby Ferrari'. Eventually, however, it was felt that time was running out for the trusty 65-degree V6 engine. By 1973, it was the best part of 10 years since the first Dino road car concept had been unveiled.

It was time for the Dino image to go up a gear, but the net result was a car which, ever since its inception, has been the focal point of more debate and disagreement than probably any other Ferrari in history.

The Dino 308GT4 was soberly styled by Bertone, thereby becoming the first Ferrari-made car in 20 years not to carry a Pininfarina bodyshell. Following so soon after the shapely 246, it was slammed as an awkward and uninspired shape, but it was destined to mature gradually in people's perceptions over the next decade and is now regarded as one of the more under-rated machines to emerge from Maranello.

The initial colour brochure inadvertently reflected the awkwardness felt about the 308GT4 almost from its first public appearance. 'The experience of Ferrari in the smaller GT car range', read the English translation of what the publicists were attempting to say. It sounds better in Italian – *L'esperienza Ferrari nella Granturismo di piccola serie* – but only just! It was difficult to know what they meant because, however one sliced it, the Dino had now well and truly grown up. You could say that the beautiful duckling had turned into an ugly swan.

The general disappointment was, in part, because of the brief given to Bertone. Though the car was to retain the compact dimensions of the 246, it was thought desirable to add two 'occasional' seats in the rear. This was less to accommodate people than to counter criticism of the first Dino that when driver and passenger were seated there was nowhere inside the car to put a coat, a briefcase or a handbag. Designing Ferrari's first mid-engined 2 + 2 was going to be a tough job, whoever did it.

Why Bertone were commissioned remains the subject of conjecture. The association between Ferrari and Pininfarina runs deep; Enzo Ferrari and Battista Pininfarina first worked together in 1951 and today Sergio Pininfarina is a director of Ferrari. Fiat, on the other hand, have long had a policy of spreading their outside design commissions to make the best use of available talent – and, it is suggested, to stop one firm getting too comfortable and complacent with fat Fiat contracts... Perhaps this thinking prevailed at the time of the Fiat-Ferrari accord, when the V6 Dino's successor was being planned.

Undoubtedly another factor was the Fiat Dino, which was available with two-seater convertible and 2 + 2 coupe bodies. The Bertone coupe was an altogether more successful design than Pininfarina's spider, and when, after the expansion of the Maranello works, the Fiats were assembled alongside the 246s, Ferrari had direct experience of dealing with Bertone.

Whatever the reason, Bertone's was a one-off contract, much to the disappointment of Nuccio Bertone, the senior of Turin's consultants, who recently was still using a 308GT4 as his everyday transport.

At the heart of this new Dino was a brand new V8 engine – Ferrari's first for a road car. The F106AL engine was, in essence,

Bertone's controversial styling of the 308GT4 is probably seen at its best from a relatively high angle such as this. Note the simplified front-end treatment of this car with just two light units recessed into the narrow bumper and nothing flanking the horizontal-bar grille beneath.

The high waistline is very evident in this side view of an early 308GT4. As on the car pictured above, the wheel retaining nuts are hidden behind small covers.

Early production 308GT4s were equipped with a wide and deep grille with twin light units each side beneath the recessed headlamps. Side repeater flashers are mounted forward of the front wheels.

related to the 90-degree V8 Formula 1 engine designed by Angelo Bellei a decade earlier which powered John Surtees to the 1964 World Championship. With a bore and stroke of 81 × 71mm (the same as the 12-cylinder 365 model), this 2,926cc unit was cast in light alloy with shrunken-in cylinder liners and fitted with a five-bearing crankshaft. The twin overhead camshafts were driven by internally toothed, flexible belts, and activated inclined valves by means of thimble tappets. Wet-sump lubrication was employed, circulation of the lubricant being looked after by a gear-driven pump, while the system also included an oil cooler as standard. Ignition was by two Marelli distributors to the single spark plugs per cylinder and the 12-volt electrical system employed an alternator and transistorized regulator.

The engine was fitted with four twin-choke Weber 40DCNF carburettors and, with a compression ratio of 8.8:1, produced a nominal 255bhp at 7,700rpm. Its dry weight was quoted as 1,365kg (3,009lb). The claimed maximum speed at the time of its announcement was 148mph. Its main rivals on the market at that time were the Lamborghini Urraco, slightly lighter at 1,308kg (2,884lb) and producing 143mph from its 2.4-litre V8; the Maserati Merak, offering 149mph from a 2.9-litre V6 with a weight of 1,320kg (2,910lb) and, inevitably, Porsche's latest corresponding model, the 1,075kg (2,370lb) 911 Carrera with 210bhp and a top speed a whisker short of 150mph.

The transversely mounted 3-litre V8 engine and transmission, a package which would outlive the 308GT4 to power the next generation of Pininfarina-styled GTBs and their derivatives.

The new Dino's transmission configuration was virtually identical to that in the superseded 246, the engine sitting atop the five-speed transmission/final drive unit. In the 308GT4, power is transmitted from the clutch to the gearbox through a series of three step-down gears, with a quill shaft transmitting the drive into the box itself, absorbing torsional vibration as it does so.

Drive out to the wheels is by means of solid drive-shafts using Birfield-Rzeppa constant-velocity joints, those on the inboard end being of the sliding type. Outboard ventilated disc brakes are fitted all round – ½in diameter front, 10¾in rear – while the handbrake operates on small drums fitted within the rear discs. A tandem master cylinder actuates the dual-circuit hydraulic system and a Bonaldi vacuum servo provides assistance.

Ferrari recommended Michelin XWX 205/70 VR14 radial tyres, with similarly rated Goodyear Grand Prix 800s as an alternative. Standard equipment Campagnolo light-alloy wheels were supplemented by a 'get-you-home' spare tucked away in a well behind the front radiator duct.

The basic Dino 246 chassis frame had been judged extremely strong and satisfactory, so it was only to be expected that Ferrari

Driver's-eye view of the instrument panel of a right-hand-drive 308GT4. Fuel, oil pressure and water and oil temperature gauges are housed alongside the rev-counter and speedometer, with a centrally mounted small clock partly obscured by the steering wheel hub.

Recessed cushions between the side bolsters of the front seats offer good lateral and thigh support. Controls for the electric window lifts are two of several items mounted on the central chassis backbone.

The 308GT4 is a 2 + 2, but only just, minimal space behind the front seats making those behind suitable only for children for anything other than short journeys. Again the cushions are sensibly recessed.

Later 308GT4s have a modified grille with bars extending over the two auxiliary lights, which consequently tend to be cleaned less frequently. Unlike the earlier cars, this one proudly displays the Ferrari Prancing Horse emblem on the nose.

would adopt a similar layout for the bigger-engined model. Based on a square platform of oval steel tubes, parallel members extend fore-and-aft from this structure to support front and rear suspensions and engine mountings. The extensions are stiffened not only by cross-members, but also by oval tube braces from the corners of the main perimeter frame.

The central frame is sheeted in with a steel and glass-fibre floor panel, but without the additional undertray which the 246 had welded to the upper and lower edges of the perimeter frame in order to form a strong, rigid box section. The flip side of that feature on the earlier car had been a proneness to internal condensation and rusting. The revised approach on the 308 is not only lighter but also appreciably stronger.

Mounted on to the 308's base structure are two box-like cages, front and rear. The front one provides mounting points for the upper and lower wishbones and coil springs, while the larger one at the back provides the engine support frame in addition to picking up the suspension. The suspension configuration all round is virtually identical to that of the 246, with double wishbones pressed from heavy-gauge steel sheet.

'2+2' the 308GT4 might have been touted as, but only children – young, small children – could squeeze into the rear seats for anything more than a quick sprint round the block. Anyway, the seats are absurdly upright in position, with next to no support under the knees.

In the front, the 308GT4 is a different matter altogether, accommodation being generous and well laid out. There is more internal storage room available in the V8-engined car, with a

Mark Newton's 308GT4 has the comparative rarity of a sliding roof. Other than the licence disc in the bottom corner, the circular decals on the screen denote membership of the Ferrari Owner's Club for the past three years.

Behind the radiator and its plumbing and ahead of the screen bulkhead there is not a lot of space, but sufficient to house a 'get you home' spare wheel and tyre, the accessibility of which is good.

good-sized glovebox, pockets in the doors, plus handy little cubby holes behind the rear seats. As far as luggage is concerned, there is room for a soft bag under the bonnet, and limited additional storage space behind the engine at the rear of the car.

Most testers were disappointed to find that there was a trace of the frustrating 'Italian' driving position in the 308, although if you juggled about with the seat's fore/aft and backrest adjustment, it was almost possible to 'tune out' this irritating quirk. A more enduring annoyance was the markedly offset pedal layout and the heavy clutch pedal, which also had a very long travel, a factor that would prove wearisome to the 308GT4 owner when motoring in traffic.

Apart from these reservations and criticisms, the general layout of the cockpit is attractive and workable, very like the original 246 in fact, although the instrument panel is angled in towards the driver at its outer extremities. Immediately ahead of the driver is a matching speedometer and rev-counter, sandwiching three smaller dials, the oil pressure and water temperature gauges and a clock. On the outside of the facia are the oil temperature and fuel gauges, this latter pair inevitably obscured by the wheel rim, making one wonder whether the clock's pre-eminent position in the centre of the layout should

A rear luggage compartment of reasonable proportions and sensible shape is a strong practical feature of the 308GT4. Both the compartment and its self-supporting lid are trimmed.

The 3-litre engine is comparatively accessible beneath the lid of the more forward rear compartment, although all but the most rudimentary of tasks is best left to a Ferrari specialist.

have been relinquished in favour of one of its more important colleagues.

The heating and ventilation systems on the 308GT4 attracted a great deal of criticism, being primitive and inadequate on a car which was priced at £8,339.76p in the UK before one began leafing through the list of optional extras. As far as the heater was concerned, Ferrari had used a water mix system which, inevitably, was extremely slow to respond to changes in adjustment and, moreover, inconsistent and unpredictable in effect. The distribution of the hot/cold air, with separate controls for each footwell, allowed either full flow to the screen or a split between screen and footwells; there was no facility to aim it all at the floor, resulting in complaints that the system had not been thought out properly from the start. Add to that the noisy and inadequate single-speed fan and you had a testimony to the amount of leeway in detail finish Ferrari still had to make up...

As the ventilation was so hopeless, the only real option was to pay out another £374 for air conditioning. Perhaps there was some method in this aspect of Ferrari's madness...

A generous-size rear screen offers acceptable rear vision from the driver's seat. Later 308GT4s have the model designation on the luggage compartment lid with the Ferrari name-plate either above or below the rear number-plate.

In fact, taken as a whole, the 308GT4's level of equipment was less than acceptable for a car costing this sort of money in 1974. Perhaps we've all taken for granted the host of extras which are accepted as basic equipment on luxury cars in the 1980s – or perhaps the pricing structure of the Dino 308GT4 really was as unreasonable as it seemed at the time. Either way, this chunky, rather boxy Maranello challenger did not really strike the right chord. But once behind the wheel, you had no doubt: this was a proper Ferrari, never mind the fact that it only had eight cylinders at a time when most people were obsessed with the idea that 'proper' Ferraris had 12. But the attempt to propagate the Dino name as a separate, individual marque, and the 308GT4's bland styling, meant that it was regarded with a degree of caution by Ferrari enthusiasts.

When the more emotionally styled, Pininfarina-bodied 308GTB exploded onto the scene in 1975, many people believed this was the true 'child of 246', and the 308GT4 thereafter took something of a back seat in the Maranello range. In 1976, discreetly and without fuss, Ferrari motifs appeared on the 308GT4. This subtle but significant change was accompanied by a new grille with a more aggressive, spaced-out latticework pattern.

As far as motor sport was concerned, the 308GT4 was effectively a non-starter, although Luigi Chinetti's North American Racing Team (winner of the Ferrari marque's last-ever Le Mans victory in 1965) turned up at La Sarthe for the 1974 24-hour race with a specially-prepared 308 racer on behalf of owner Bill Schanbacher. Outwardly it may have looked 'the business',

Bertone, having been issued with a number of design restraints before styling the 308GT4, found full freedom of expression in creating the Ferrari 308-based Rainbow in 1976. So named because it was convertible from coupe to spider, for 'rain' or 'sun' use, from the driver's seat, it was built strictly as a show car on a wheelbase 10cm shorter than that of the 308GT4.

with its wider wheels, racing tyres, wide arches, air dam and rear wing, but it proved hopelessly off-the-pace in the hands of Jean-Louis Lafosse and Giancarlo Gagliardi. Delayed by early braking problems, it eventually came to a halt out on the circuit with a broken clutch.

The Ferrari 308GT4 rolled on in production until December 1980, only minor specification changes punctuating the final four years of its life.

Italy's sliding scale of car taxation, which heavily penalized those with an engine capacity in excess of 2 litres, allied to continuing concern about the oil crisis, gave rise to a 208GT4, which was introduced at the Geneva Motor Show in 1975. Powered by a 66.8 × 71mm, 1,991cc F106C version of the V8, developing 170bhp at 7,700rpm, it had a claimed top speed of 137mph. Fitted with a lower final drive ratio and running on narrower Michelin XDX tyres, it was distinguishable by having only a single exhaust and the absence of foglights at either side of the now-silver (rather than matt black) grille.

Finally, mention should be made of the Bertone styling exercise, based on the GT4, which was unveiled at the 1976 Turin Show. Clearly concerned that the GT4 had been criticized for its conservative design, the coachbuilder produced a wedge-shaped design exercise titled 'Rainbow', the lines of which were severely angular, with not a curve to be seen. Its most distinctive feature was a 'targa' top which could be swung down behind the seats while the driver remained in the cockpit.

In its eight-year production run, a total of 2,826 GT4s were produced, some 547 of which found their way into the UK. Although eclipsed by the 308GTBs from 1975 onwards, there was no equivalent in the range until the Mondial 8 came on the scene five years later. By that time, Ferrari and Pininfarina had worked out a way of scheming a 2 + 2 within the confined central-engined package to far better effect.

Inevitably, by this stage, many early GT4s had found their way into the hands of owners who were financially ill-equipped to prevent their mechanical and bodywork deterioration. At the turn of the decade, a lot of tatty, neglected examples could be picked up on the secondhand market for the proverbial song. Only in the mid-1980s, when Ferrari enthusiasts suddenly woke up to how under-valued they were, did the 308GT4s begin to gain acceptance as excellent, appealing and worthwhile investments.

Handicapped by its own identity, outward looks and the 1974 fuel crisis, the GT4 only became acknowledged as a collector's piece more than a decade after its hesitant debut.

CHAPTER 6

308GTB and GTS

Beautiful classics

The Paris Motor Show of 1975 heralded the arrival of the first of a series of classic Ferraris, the progeny of which is still much appreciated as we approach the end of the 1980s. This was the first of the 308GTBs, the bodywork design of which reverted to Pininfarina. Manufactured by Scaglietti, it was built in glass-fibre until mid-1977 and subsequently in steel. Delicious is the only word to describe it...

The GTB was the answer to those Ferrari customers who had begged for a more sporting development of the original Dino 246 concept. Truly, it could now be said that Dino had grown up, but the Ferrari's Fiat management had by this stage accepted the popular belief that Dinos were somehow not 'proper' Ferraris and the 308GTBs were tagged as Ferraris from the outset. Their technical lineage owed a great deal to the GT4, notably the well-proven tubular chassis, on to which the shapely new body panels were mounted.

With no pretence as anything but a two-seater, the 308GTB reverted to the 92.1in wheelbase of the original 246GT, and the engine, producing the same 255bhp output as the GT4, now had the benefit of dry-sump lubrication. In this form it was designated F106AB.

Instantly, Ferrari enthusiasts were enthralled, the 308GTB's immediate appeal wiping away any unfortunate memories attaching to the GT4. In *Autosport*, John Bolster wrote: 'When Ferrari replaced the much-loved Dino 246 with the 308GT4 2+2, there were murmurs that much of the very special character of the original car had been lost. The new V8 engine was a vast improvement on the V6, which was rather low on torque in the lower-middle ranges, but Bertone's body was less sporting than

its immediate predecessor. Now Ferrari have produced an additional model which has all the glamour of the Dino 246 plus the extra horsepower and, above all, the massive torque of the V8.'

It was a sentiment echoed by most of Bolster's fellow scribes, although *Motor Sport's* Denis Jenkinson sounded what amounted to a cautionary note. In his opinion, *real* Ferraris had front-mounted, big-capacity V12 engines and, although the shrill little Dino 246 could truly be regarded as 'son of Ferrari', the 308GTB was rather characterless and bland for his taste. In praising the amount of power and torque available, Jenks bemoaned the fact that 'the V8 engine doesn't sing to itself like the little V6 Dino engine, so you might as well let it burble away at 3,500rpm... When Fiat took over the Ferrari empire, Enzo Ferrari said "that's fine, you look after production and I can concentrate on the motor racing, which is all I have ever really enjoyed". In the Ferrari 308GTB we have a modern, efficient, effective and first-class automobile, but somehow it does not exude the magic of Enzo Ferrari. The idiosyncracies and character that Enzo Ferrari put into his cars seems to have been discreetly swept away by the dead hand of Fiat.'

That was regarded as fighting stuff in the mid-1970s, and in retrospect it seems a rather harsh judgment. Ferrari's main line production would henceforth be based on 308GTB derivatives and, although beyond question the car was refined, it would be made more powerful and the range significantly widened in the years that followed. Meanwhile, the first of these delectable central-engined, V8 two-seaters was a symbolic re-affirmation of Maranello's intention to build driver's cars, blending fine

47

Elegance returned to the Ferrari Dino line with the introduction of the 308GTB in 1975, a two-seater coupe which recalled the curvaceousness of Pininfarina's earlier 246GT.

The soft curves of the 308GTB are unimpaired by the discreet chin and tail spoilers which contribute considerably to the car's dynamic stability.

performance into a package which handled, steered and braked as well as anything available on the market. True, they were not 'hairy chested' sports cars in the idiom of the 1950s and early 1960s, but discerning buyers wanted more from their supercars in the mid-1970s, and the 308GTBs were out to satisfy just that requirement...

Within the cockpit, the GTB hardly has room for a set of road maps, let alone even the most pliable travelling bag. The two footwells are separated by a central tunnel in which runs the pipework taking coolant from the engine to the front-mounted radiator, in addition to the gearchange and handbrake linkages.

From the outset, the GTB's fuel consumption figures were claimed to be in the region of 18 to 22mpg, but most road-testers were hard pressed to improve on 15mpg. Fitted with Michelin XWX 205/70 VR14 radial tyres and a 3.71:1 (17/63) rear axle ratio, a 7,000rpm limit produced 41, 59, 83, 112 and 156.6mph in the five gears. Maximum torque was 210lb/ft at 5,000rpm.

The GTB is only half an inch wider than the GT4, but 3½in lower. Its minimal wheel movement makes for a choppy ride at low speeds, when the car seems super-sensitive to bumps and surface ripples, but once really moving the chassis and suspension are perfectly matched and instill considerable con-

Contrasting seat trim is repeated on the doors of this early 308GTB. Note the narrowness of the footwells as a result of the intrusion of the front wheelarches into the corners of the cockpit, but a rest has thoughtfully been provided for the clutch foot.

A compact main instrument panel on the 308GTB houses just the fuel, water temperature and oil pressure gauges along with the rev-counter and speedometer, the oil temperature gauge and clock being repositioned and partially obscured between steering wheel rim and driver's door on early cars, although they were to be relocated in a centre console on later variants.

The high-tail bodywork gives this early 308GTB an almost aggressively powerful appearance from such a low angle. However, the single exhaust tailpipe confirms that this is the least powerful version of the series.

Two views into the engine compartment of a 308GTS. Note the tight fit of the air cleaner beneath the lid of the compartment, also the tie bar linking the body/chassis to the rearmost engine cam cover. The tops of the coil spring/damper units can just be seen protruding into the sides of the engine bay.

fidence in the user. The car not only feels safe and secure, but soaks up those bumps impressively, with no inclination towards pitching or floating.

By any contemporary standards, the GTB was quick, sprinting from rest to 60mph in 6.8sec and with a top speed of 150mph. The other side of the coin remained the car's tremendous flexibility, it being quite capable of pulling away from 1,200rpm in fifth without hesitation or stuttering.

The GTB's gearchange was praised by most commentators as a significant improvement over that in the GT4. The clutch, however, continued to attract a lot of criticism for being stiff and hard to operate, the gears being particularly difficult to select when the transmission was cold.

The low-geared steering has 3.3 turns lock-to-lock, but while this produces an unrealistic turning circle (in the region of 40ft) it contributes to the superb balance and feel at high speed. Basically, the GTB has a touch of built-in understeer, but it is easy to invoke a touch of oversteer to compensate for any loss of front-end grip. Everyone agrees that it is a delight to drive.

However, contemporary British road test reports point to more fundamental problems compromising Maranello's market opportunities. When Anthony Curtis tested the Maranello Concessionaires GTB demonstrator for *Motor* magazine in 1976, he found, at first acquaintance, that the handling was dreadful. He couldn't understand why the car understeered to an unacceptable degree, displayed worrying instability under heavy braking and 'bottomed out' badly on its suspension. He referred the matter back to Maranello Concessionaires, 'who listed our complaints, checked the car over and returned it to us with new front dampers, adjusted rear ones and correctly set steering geometry'. From then on it was fine...

Meanwhile, my colleagues at *Motor Sport* had found other shortcomings which, whilst not affecting the overall appeal of the GTB from a purist driving point of view, were exactly the kind of problems which *didn't* crop up on rival Porsches of the time. On a long run to visit Editor Bill Boddy in Wales, Jenks found that 'our' 308GTB leaked like the proverbial sieve. Water not only poured in through the top of the driver's door, but also cascaded into the boot at the rear of the engine. We also bemoaned the fact that water collects on the flat engine cover and, when you raise it

The spare wheel and tyre effectively fill all the available space in the front of this 308. Note the strip of cushioning material provided between the top of the radiator and the front-hinged body panel.

Exhaust gases take a circuitous route before finally emerging through the single tailpipe on the left side of the tail.

(even just to take a briefcase out of the rearward, zip cover-protected luggage compartment) you end up dumping half a gallon of water all over the engine and, more particularly, the distributor.

Inside, not too much thought had been given to the instrumentation. Designing speedometers and rev-counters with black dials and dark green needles was just confusing, because even though the tips of the needles were white, they became virtually impossible to see once they were lined up with the white markings on the dial face. As for the rev-counter, the figures vary from white to orange, to dark red, on a black background as you progress up the rev range... Jenks also commented on the binnacle over the instruments that reflected the sunshine 'up on to the windscreen to form a nice fuzzy glare in front of the driver's face'.

Just as the 246GT spawned the GTS, so there was to be a GTS spider version of the 308GTB, which was received with similar enthusiasm on its introduction in 1977.

This three-quarter view of the 308GTS reveals that a measure of driver visibility is provided through the louvred panels behind the roll hoop, despite their 'solid' appearance from certain angles.

Finally, he lambasted the design of the stalk on the left-hand side of the steering column, which controlled the lights. Rotating the end of this stalk put on the side and tail lights, while moving the lever down a notch activated electric motors which raised the hidden headlights on dipped beam. 'Flick the lever up a notch and you were back on "dipped", which was fine, except that I have a simple brain that thinks a lever control moving upwards should put things up and a lever moving downwards should put things down. Not on a Ferrari. In the heat of the moment, such as overtaking in a hurry, flicking the lever inadvertently the wrong way not only does not give you full beam, but takes away the "dipped" beam and the headlamps fold smartly out of sight. Presumably, if Ferrari owners live long enough, they will get used to this very dangerous lack of "fail-safe thinking".'

At the 1977 Frankfurt Motor Show, Pininfarina's latest variation on the current theme, the GTS spider, rounded off the range to put the 308 back where the 246 had been five years earlier.

As with the 246GTS, the new spider had a roll hoop concealed behind the cockpit and the rear quarter windows were blanked off, in this case by black louvred panels. One mechanical difference from the GTB was the use, for reasons of underbonnet space, of the wet-sump engine from the GT4.

The most interesting aspect of this superbly-conceived open two-seater was the removable padded glass-fibre roof section which, in the words of *Car and Driver*, could be removed 'in a matter of 15 seconds and with less effort than it takes to lift a couple of grocery bags into the back of a station wagon'.

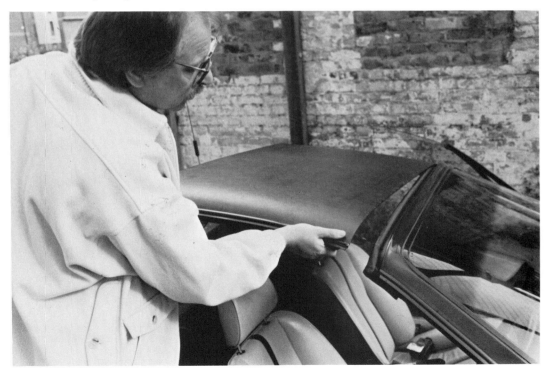

Removing the glass-fibre roof panel from a GTS is a straightforward job requiring only a matter of seconds. When removed the top is placed in a weatherproof bag and stored behind the seats.

The 308GTS in fair-weather guise. Note the neat door-release handle, also the 'envelope' for odds and ends attached to the fully trimmed door. The front-hinged louvred panels behind the doors swivel outwards when released by a key at their rear end.

Restored immaculately, this 308GTS is probably in better and more durable condition bodily than when it first left the factory.

Luxurious rugs protect the floor mats of the restored GTS. Enzo Ferrari may think that some of his customers go 'over the top' in restoring and preserving their cars, but can they really be blamed for completing a little unfinished business?

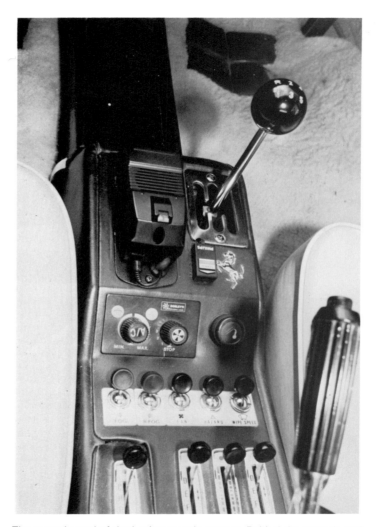

The control panel of the businessman's express. Behind the controls and cradle for the in-car telephone are the toggle switches for the fog lamps, the fan, the hazard lights and the wipers, plus a quartet of slide controls for the heating and ventilation equipment.

Two simple swivel clips secured the panel and it could be safely tucked away behind the seats, encased in a waterproof vinyl cover if so desired. Predictably, the 308GTS was gobbled up with delight by the West Coast USA *boulevardiers* and it sold well in the USA generally.

The open-topped version and the US market were among the reasons for abandoning glass-fibre for the main bodywork and reverting to steel. Though they would be reluctant to admit it, the plastic was originally seen as a way of tackling the rust problem that affected the earlier cars, for at that time Ferrari were not equipped to offer effective corrosion protection for steel panels.

For the US market, safety regulations – and a general feeling that a 'pure' Ferrari (as this was now labelled) should not be made in glass-fibre – had already brought a run of steel-bodied GTBs. Now the GTS demanded further body strengthening to cope with the 'targa' roof. The glass-fibre bodies were also more time-consuming to manufacture, so the decision was taken to make all versions in steel. Scaglietti made the change in June 1977.

Neither the factory nor usually reliable Ferrari sources are able to ascertain precisely how many GTBs were made in glass-fibre during the first 18 months of production, but some say it could be as few as 200. Ironically, these cars – some 250lb lighter than their steel-bodied counterparts and, of course, less prone to the ravages of rust – are now the most sought-after.

Not having evolved from or for racing, the 308GTB had little to offer for top-line motor sport. At the 1977 Geneva Show, Pininfarina played about with a 'competition' design exercise, spoiling the lines of a standard GTB by tacking on unsightly and unpainted aluminium flared arches, plus tail and roof spoilers. It progressed no further than its show stand, but there had already been rumours of much-modified 308GTBs running on the roads near Maranello, or pounding round the Fiorano test track, giving rise to speculation in the Italian racing magazine *Autosprint* that an ambitious twin Garrett turbo machine was being developed for Giampiero Moretti and movie star Paul Newman to drive at Le Mans in 1977. It was suggested that Moretti had commissioned former Ferrari engineer Giacomo Caliri, who now operated his own Milan-based freelance design studio, Smartauto, to produce this fascinating variant. However, nothing seemed to be happening on this front until, towards the end of the following year, Carlo Facetti came up with a Group 5 'silhouette'

Beautiful yet functional. The air scoops along the body sides of the GTB and GTS not only contribute to the success of the overall styling theme, they ensure that temperatures within the engine bay and around the inboard rear brakes are kept at a tolerable level.

308GTB. This was not a serious long-term proposition, although Facetti was to toy with versions of the 308 and by 1981 had produced a fearsomely fast twin-turbo version developing some 840bhp, which actually got in amongst the Porsches at Daytona. It contested a programme of World Championship sports car events throughout 1981, but never developed sufficient reliability to match its power.

In rallying, Ferrari's indirect involvement was with the Lancia Stratos (which used the Dino V6 engine), but some wealthy privateers did campaign 308GTBs in European tarmac events. Notable among them was the French Ferrari distributor Charles Pozzi, who provided a Group 4-specification car for the mercurial Jean-Claude Andruet in 1981 and 1982.

Andruet's car, a glass-fibre-bodied model with a Kugelfischer fuel-injected engine that developed 310bhp, gave its best on the Tour de Corse and came close to winning this Corsican World Championship rally in 1982. He went on to win the Tour de France that year, while Italian Antonio Tognana was victorious in two Italian rounds of the European Rally Championship with his GTB.

Meanwhile, in world markets, the 308GTB and GTS flourished. There were, however, some quality control problems, and in America the car's performance was deteriorating with the increasing restriction of exhaust emissions. At first, the US models – which were fitted with the GT4's wet-sump engine – lost only 15bhp compared to the European spec. They were quoted as developing 240bhp at 6,600rpm, 1,100rpm less than

Access to the fuel filler cap on the 308GTS is by releasing the left-hand hinged louvred panel. This is also the way to clean the otherwise concealed small windows behind the doors.

On the GTB and GTS a single front-hinged panel exposes both the engine compartment and the fully trimmed luggage area behind it, the latter being protected by a flexible cover. Twin pneumatic springs hold the panel aloft.

Pininfarina hinted at the way ahead with this styling study which appeared at the 1977 Turin Show. Certain of the aerodynamic aids would find their way into production, but not the rivet-secured wing extensions over the wheels.

the original. Later 'federalized' versions were down much more.

It should be said that all of the factory's power figures – European and US – are somewhat questionable. The original 255bhp might more realistically have been around 230. What is certain, though, is that earlier cars for both markets were more powerful than later ones and that the American ones suffered badly as they went into the 1980s. That's clear from the road test figures, for while a European car was good for 150mph and 0-60mph in less than 7sec, *Road & Track* recorded only 132mph and 9.4sec for a US-spec GTB.

Apart from emission control equipment, American versions differed from European models in having twin distributors and some detail body changes.

When the 308GTB first arrived on the UK market it was priced at £10,501 inclusive of car tax and VAT. Standard equipment included electric window lifts, tinted glass, laminated windscreen (with a tinted upper band), heated rear window and leather upholstery. Options included air conditioning, metallic paint finish and slightly wider-rimmed wheels (though carrying standard-sized tyres).

In the USA, the initial price was $28,500 (East Coast) and $29,525 (West Coast), where air conditioning was wisely included as standard.

For Italy alone, 2-litre 208 versions of both the GTB and GTS were offered, using the same power unit as the 208GT4.

The GTB and GTS represented Ferrari's most serious effort

The production Ferrari Dinos have not had an extensive competition career, but in England there is a race series for road-going Ferraris and Tony Worswick for one has demonstrated the versatility of the 308/328 series by both racing and rallying them.

to manufacture Porsche-beating mid-engined sports cars on what, for them, could be termed volume scale. The Dino 246 had been a super jewel, but in many ways it was a missed opportunity; it suffered from poor durability and a market that perhaps did not fully appreciate what was being sold as a Dino. Bertone's effort with the 308GT4 had been worthy enough, but the car's styling failed to catch the mood of the times. The 308GTB had everything a Ferrari fan of the 1970s could dream about. It was, truly, a gorgeous car.

CHAPTER 7

Mondial 8

Fuel injection introduced

Preliminary outlines of a 2 + 2 design to replace the GT4 were considered as far back as 1976, but Pininfarina's chief stylist Leonardo Fiorovanti was adamant that the job could not be done properly unless a slight increase in wheelbase was sanctioned to produce some semblance of room for rear seat occupants. The result was a 10cm (3.9in) lengthening and the end result of the design process, the Mondial 8, was finally unveiled to the waiting world at the 1980 Geneva Motor Show.

The name Mondial echoed memories of the original Pininfarina-designed Scaglietti-built two-seater which was powered by a version of the 2-litre four-cylinder unit which Alberto Ascari had used in the Formula 2 Type 500 to win the World Championship in 1952 and 1953.

However, whilst this original Mondial had direct competition lineage, and indeed enjoyed some competition outings, mainly in the hands of privateers, the 308GTB's younger sister was a gentle, almost mellow grand tourer in its original guise. It certainly was not a high-performance machine in the accepted Ferrari sense of the word, and it attracted some criticism both for what some regarded as its awkward lines and for its comparatively leisurely performance.

It was a classic example of Ferrari losing out whatever it did. In the past, its emphasis on out-and-out high performance, with little in the way of compromise, had drawn the critics' attention. The company was accused of having too narrow a commercial outlook. Now, the Mondial 8 made a very real effort at expanding the marque's appeal, but the slight 'softening' of the high-performance image was damned by the purists.

While the family resemblance to the curvaceous GTB was

obvious, the most crucially significant aspect of the Mondial 8 was the care and attention to detail which had gone into the business of making the car. Bruised by criticism of poor finish and durability throughout the 1970s, Fiat now realized that its prestige shop window really did have to get on top of its quality shortcomings if it was to get a sniff of the Porsche/Mercedes market. This was a particularly important priority in the USA which, at the time, accounted for upwards of 35% of the entire annual Maranello factory output.

The Mondial's main bodyshell was manufactured from pre-treated Zincrometal steel, with the doors, bonnet and boot lids, roof and wing panels made in an alloy called Alusingen. An up-to-the-minute high-tech welding facility was installed at Scaglietti to assemble the bodyshells. They were treated with a pure zinc pre-processing preparation to which was added a PVC-based anti-abrasion undercoat.

Beneath the skin, the Mondial 8 conformed to familiar Ferrari design techniques, the bodyshell mounted on the classic tube-frame base, which made more use of steel sheet reinforcement than on the GTB. The engine and gearbox were mounted on a separate subframe, which simply dropped away from the underside of the car for ease of maintenance. The design included centre-point steering and anti-dive built into the front suspension. The rear of the cabin was obviously considerably more spacious than that in the GT4, although it could by no means be described as generous. You could squeeze in a couple of adults for the shortest of journeys, but it was fine for kids.

Sadly, the engine's performance was strangled. In producing what was intended to be such a cosmopolitan motor car, Ferrari

In styling the Mondial 8 Pininfarina requested and was granted an extension of 10cm over the wheelbase of the 308GT4 in order to combine adequate four-seater accommodation with an acceptable exterior profile. The deep grilles over the side air intakes were something of a shock after the neat flutes of the GTB/GTS series, but were made less obtrusive when they were later changed to body colour instead of black.

Twin headlamps in the pop-up nacelles of the Mondial are a reminder of the layout adopted for the GT4 whereas single light units suffice for the GTB/GTS series. Pininfarina adopted a different grille treatment for the four-seater car.

was obliged to cater for the stringent US anti-emission laws, and the rest of the buying public would have to take the Mondial 8 to basically the same specification, or buy something else.

For the new F106B engine, out went the Weber carburettors and in came the Bosch K-Jetronic electronic injection system, which had been introduced a year earlier on the big front-engined 400i V12. The Mondial 8 engine specification also included Marelli Digiplex electronic ignition, which made available eight different spark advance curves, better suiting the needs of the twin-overhead-camshaft V8 engine. There was also a new check control monitor that kept a watching brief on liquid levels and lighting systems, flashing up a battery of warning lights every time the engine was fired up, then going out if everything was in order.

The power output was down from 240/255bhp DIN to a paltry 214bhp at 6,600rpm, the torque reduced from 209lb/ft at 5,000rpm on the European-market GTBs to 179lb/ft at 4,600 rpm. On the credit side, however, was a significantly lighter gear change, still guided by that nice metal 'clackety-clack' gate, and a clutch that didn't need a superhuman effort to depress.

However, for me it is the interior of the Mondial 8 which makes the biggest impression. Frankly, I can take or leave the styling; its proportions seem all out of step, being too long for its width. But the care and attention to detail of the interior trim and fittings bears immediate witness to the firm's intention to improve the quality of the product.

The driver's seat is superbly upholstered and trimmed in leather, though perhaps a trifle narrow for the author's figure. Among the high-quality carpet and the leather trim extending upwards to the door panels and facia, I can find no trace of shoddy workmanship. In my judgment, the overall finish, inside and out, approaches the sort of level we have been used to expecting from Porsche.

The adjustable steering column allows even the tallest driver to use the seat's rearward adjustment to achieve a comfortable relationship between wheel and pedals. Headroom is excellent and elbow room more than adequate, although the intrusion of the wheelarch obviously means that the pedals remain offset.

The Mondial's V8 certainly impressed everybody with its flexibility. The fuel-injected engine fires up without any trace of

The four-tailpipe exhaust system of the fuel-injected engine are flanked by a pair of fog lights recessed into the body skirt. As on the GT4, separate lids are provided for the engine and luggage compartments of the Mondial.

spitting or coughing, just a pleasant blend of deep rasping and mechanical whirring. And, notwithstanding its lack of 'grunt', the two-valves-per-cylinder engine just revs and revs. At one end of the scale its flexibility and docility allows you to chunter along at about 20mph in fifth gear, or you can get the rev-counter needle hurtling round its dial.

The Mondial 8's figures – 0-60mph in just over 7sec, 100mph in just over 20sec – certainly do not qualify the machine as a supercar and its performance limitations can be found in fourth gear when it begins to get a bit breathless above 115mph. After that, the long slog up towards its claimed maximum of 150mph looks a bit like tackling Everest without any previous experience at mountain-climbing. Some magazines at the time cast serious doubts over the Mondial's ability to haul itself over 140mph.

There is a perceptible degree of roll from the coil spring/unequal-length wishbone suspension and one gains the initial impression that the Michelin TRX radials do a good job ironing out the bumps. However, when I was driving a Mondial 8 in the summer of 1981 I used it to visit Silverstone for the pre-British Grand Prix test session and its sleek lines inevitably attracted the curiosity of Lotus boss Colin Chapman, who asked if he could drive it for a couple of 'squirts' up Silverstone's Club Straight.

Proud of the standards of ride he had instilled into his own company's road cars – the Eclat and Esprit – Colin took quite a huffy view of the Mondial's ride over even the slightest bump. He grudgingly accepted that the steering was 'quite reasonable' and simply loved the yowl from the wound-up V8. But, taken as a whole, he thought the chassis behaviour was quite average. 'Not in the same class as a Lotus, my lad' he said, as he closed the driver's door and strode back into the pit lane...

Colin's remarks are interesting, but merely testify to his obsession with excellence, and should not be taken as a damning indictment of the Mondial's handling. By the standards of the time it was really excellent, and although it did not offer the same razor-sharpness of the two-seater GTB, it was forgiving and relaxing to drive. There was no fuss when you were motoring in the Mondial, which was – and remains – a true grand tourer, rather than a hairy-chested sports car.

True, if you make the mistake of running into a sweeping corner on a trailing throttle you might emerge a trifle disappoin-

Reasonable four-seater accommodation is provided in this early Mondial. The introduction of this model marked a considerable step forwards for Ferrari in the quality of interior trim and finish.

ted – and wide of the apex – with the ensuing understeer. In that respect, it takes a little time to become fully acquainted with its reassuring sure-footedness under harsh acceleration. With right foot hard down, those Michelins really do their stuff.

The view forward from the Mondial's cockpit is fine, but true to the standards set by its stablemates, rearward visibility is just plain terrible and manoeuvring in tight spaces is complicated by the amazing omission of a nearside door mirror from the car's original standard specification.

Whilst seemingly lighter than the GTB's, the clutch/gearchange could hardly be described as feather-light and, with second gear baulking in best Maranello style, I well recall a slog round London's North Circular Road with the Mondial in a winter evening's rush hour as a real misery. Nowadays, it would be possible to do the same journey with less stress on the M25, albeit at a consistent 35mph...

Still, the creature comforts within that leather-lined cockpit are always reassuring. The air conditioning system works with unobtrusive efficiency while the first-class stereo system and the effective windscreen wiper/washer system must also be mentioned as plus points.

On the outer right extremity of the facia, three buttons

The dashboard of the Mondial is markedly different from those of the other V8-engined cars and incorporates groups of push-button switches, twist controls and function warning lights. This is one of the earlier cars with a short central console and a steering wheel with exposed mounting nuts.

electrically unlock the rear luggage compartment lid, the engine cover and the bonnet (beneath which the spare Michelin TRX resides) while the bank of warning lights on the central console seems to me to be positioned precisely where nobody is going to notice them until too late, unless their eyes stray from the road long enough to slide another tape into the stereo system.

Just behind the gear lever are controls for the electric window lifts, the fuel filler cap and the retractable radio aerial on the Mondial's right rear flank. The headlights, of course, emerge upwards from the nose section. They match the car's performance potential.

The adoption of a digital read-out for the trip and total mileage indicators is unusual, but they blend in well with the conventional analog displays.

Aesthetically, the Mondial 8 is not everybody's cup of tea, but it has certainly freshened up that 2 + 2 concept originated by the GT4, and its price of £24,488.25p tax paid in the UK on its introduction, while expensive, was not totally outrageous. At the time, Porsche's 911 Turbo, for example, cost £27,950 and the 928S £25,251.

By the time it had been installed in the Mondial, there were few technical question marks hanging over the transverse alloy V8, mounted in unit with its five-speed gearbox. The transmission itself was substantially the same as on the GT4, although a slightly higher indirect fifth gear ratio (0.92 in place of 0.952:1) was employed plus an appreciably lower final drive – 4.063:1 (16/

The release lever for the steering column, which is adjustable both vertically and longitudinally on the Mondial. Note the different steering wheel of this later-series model.

The same car with a pouch for odds and ends between the rear seat backrests and twin air conditioning vents, an ashtray and a lighter in the extended console.

65) as opposed to the Bertone-bodied car's 3.706:1 (17/63). Taking into account the lower-profile Michelin TRXs (240/55 VR-390) replacing the 205/70VR covers on the GT4, there was a small reduction in the overall gearing from 21mph per 1,000rpm to 20.1mph on the Mondial.

Other minor, yet significant, specification changes to the gearbox included the incorporation of a circulating oil pump for improved cooling and, hopefully, reduced transmission noise. Selectors and gears had also been improved with reduced vibration and a better gearchange in mind.

For the North American market, the need to include still more emission control equipment – dual three-way catalytic convertors, air injection, exhaust gas recirculation – further stifled the injected engine's power output to 205bhp at 6,600rpm. When *Motor Trend* got its hands on a road test Mondial in November 1981, they noted that its 0-60mph time was a lazy 8.2sec without any comment. In its federalized form, it would stagger to 140mph. They remarked, 'thanks to its downhill gearing, the Mondial will generate an impressive top speed, but this...requires a certain amount of patience to achieve. The

There is room for a full-size spare wheel and tyre in the front of the Mondial as well as air conditioning equipment and fluid reservoirs. Black bumpers of 3-litre cars extend around to the wheelarches.

Mondial is no rival to the Boxer, but it is nevertheless a member of a select performance fraternity'.

In August 1982, the Mondial's performance would be boosted further by four-valve power in 'Quattrovalvole' trim, a subject which we will cover in more detail in the next chapter. Four-valves-per-cylinder took the power back to a more respectable 240bhp in European trim, but possibly the most interesting development came about at the 1984 Brussels Motor Show, where the latest fruits of Pininfarina/Scaglietti's work turned out to be a distinctive cabriolet version of the mid-engined 2+2.

The advent of the Mondial Convertible marked the arrival of the first regular production cabriolet from Ferrari since the 330/365 GTS models of the early 1970s. Weighing in almost 100lb lighter than the original fixed-head coupe, the Mondial 'QV'

Editor/writer Ray Hutton pauses for the photographer before giving the Mondial cabriolet a close look on its debut at Brussels in 1984. Like most open-top Ferraris it was an immediate success, especially on the US market.

The same car with its top raised has an unusually smooth roof line. Easy to lower, the hood slips into a compartment behind the rear seats, the backrests of which fold forward to provide extra luggage space.

cabriolet reflected considerable ingenuity on Ferrari's part in packaging a drophead arrangement without ruining the car's lines once the hood was lowered.

The cabriolet was just what was needed for cruising Sunset Boulevard, a point emphasised by *Road & Track*, who described it as 'the car for the boulevardier, the Monte Carlo or Newport Beach sportsman hard at play'. On a more serious note, *R&T* reckoned that the cabriolet's hood was definitely a two-man affair and noted that, while it folded away quite neatly, it did not drop completely below the bodyline and, as a result, rearward visibility was slightly compromised.

These minor complaints aside, it was a masterly piece of packaging, although somehow its driving position appeared to be more conspicuously far forward than it had been even on the fixed-head model. There was too much resonance and body shake, perhaps, but then that was the unquoted price one had to pay for such sizzling style...

Every owner likes to think that their Mondial will never let them down, but it is comforting to know that such a comprehensive toolkit is available for emergencies.

CHAPTER 8

308 Quattrovalvole and 328

Regaining the edge

It was inevitable that the Mondial's fuel-injected V8 would be standardized across the range and the fuel-injected 214bhp engine found its way into the GTB and GTS from March 1981. The suffix 'i' was added to their designation. Predictably, there was a furore amongst disciples of the prancing horse, disappointed by the general drop in power output, but the two-valves-per-cylinder fuel-injected cars were to have a very limited shelf-life. Within 18 months, Ferrari had come up with what was intended to be the answer. They introduced a 32-valve cylinder head for the 3-litre V8.

It is interesting to reflect on the way in which Ferrari promoted this development. If you skim through the firm's road car brochures over the decades you usually find only fleeting references to the relationship between the production cars and the racing team. However, with the Quattrovalvole models this changed, and Maranello celebrated their major 1982-model revisions with a booklet proclaiming how much knowledge had been directly derived from the racing effort over the years.

Though there was to be a 208 Turbo as a special for the Italian market only (making the most of the road tax regulations that still inflicted heavy penalties on cars with an engine capacity exceeding 2 litres), Ferrari rejected turbocharging for the 3-litre V8s.

The official reason given for choosing a four-valves-per-cylinder head for the mainstream 308s was 'in order to obtain a more valid technical result, increasing power and torque while at the same time ensuring the highest standards of reliability'. The QV engine was designated F105A.

Formula 1 experience was drawn upon to produce optimum profiles for the combustion chambers, while the valve angle was reduced to 33.5 degrees from the 46 degrees of the earlier injected engines. Power output was up again, to 240bhp, but the engine still produced peak power at 7,000rpm with the compression ratio increased from 8.8:1 to 9.2:1. The torque characteristics were improved to 191.6lb/ft at 5,000rpm and top speeds were quoted at 149.1mph for the Mondial and 158.4mph for the GTB/GTS.

The new cylinder head was manufactured from aluminium/silicon alloy, offering increased resistance to mechanical and thermal stresses. Special cast iron was employed for the valve seats, while the exhaust valves were manufactured from Nimonic alloy, well-tested by that stage on various F1 engines, but used on a production engine for the first time. Complementing the new heads were revised pistons and liners treated with the Nikasil electrochemical process.

Externally, the GTBi/GTSi QV were distinguished by a new, deeper grille, a supplementary grille atop the bonnet, a slightly different front bumper and modified alloy wheels. Inside the Mondial was to be found a new console between the seats, while the radio and air conditioning controls were also repositioned for ease of operation. The headlining was now made from a more luxurious, wool-based material.

When I tested the 308GTBi QV for *Motor Sport* in January 1983, I found myself just as impressed with the standard of interior trim and finish as I had been 18 months earlier when sampling the first of the two-valves-per-cylinder Mondial 8s. The paintwork had a lustrous quality about it and the tasteful blend of light tan and black leather in the cockpit more than

71

The Ferrari 308GTB series underwent several evolutionary changes to the cockpit as well as to the mechanical specification. This GTBi, for example, differs from earlier cars in having a black instrument panel, a different steering wheel and the clock and oil temperature gauge relocated from the facia to the front of the centre console.

matched up to the high standard of external detail finish.

Behind the wheel, some of the original grumbles remained. Any driver over 6ft tall still had about 1½in too little rearward adjustment of the driver's seat. The seat itself provided just sufficient support, without being excessively firm, but far more of an irritation was the tinted anti-dazzle strip which blended into the upper edge of the gently sloping windscreen and tended to 'chop off' my forward vision. At night, the instrument lighting continued to reflect into the windscreen, right in one's line of vision, and as that comment had previously been made in Jenks' road test of the original Dino 308GTB some seven years before, it seemed a shame that this rather fundamental problem had not been addressed.

All such ergonomic objections evaporated when we turned the ignition key to fire up the V8. Starting from cold requires no pressure on the throttle pedal at all, and the QV engine showed no reluctance to fire up on the first twist of the key, hot or cold.

On the move, two major areas of improvement struck me within the first couple of miles. Firstly, that uprated engine was so much nicer to drive slowly in traffic. Secondly, the clutch was considerably lighter than on the earlier cars. Unlike the Mondial range, the GTBi QV does not have an instantly adjustable steering column, although the rake can be changed with a spanner (a task for a dealer, incidentally, not one to be carried out by the home-based enthusiast). The instrumentation was still not as clearly calibrated as one might have liked, and the fuel gauge proved totally untrustworthy, the 308 rolling to a halt in rush-hour traffic on one unmemorable occasion, its tank almost bone

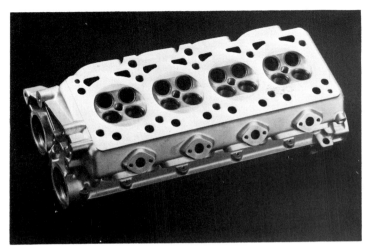

The introduction of revised cylinder heads incorporating four valves per cylinder transformed the performance of the 3-litre V8 engine and made the QV models deservedly popular. The improvement in US-market cars was particularly marked, the performance of two-valve models having been severely strangled by the essential modifications necessary to meet exhaust emissions legislation.

The four-valve breathing arrangement was carried through to the 3.2-litre engines and was later adopted for the Lancia Thema 8.32, a four-door saloon of relatively sober appearance but scintillating performance, which is referred to in more detail in Chapter 12.

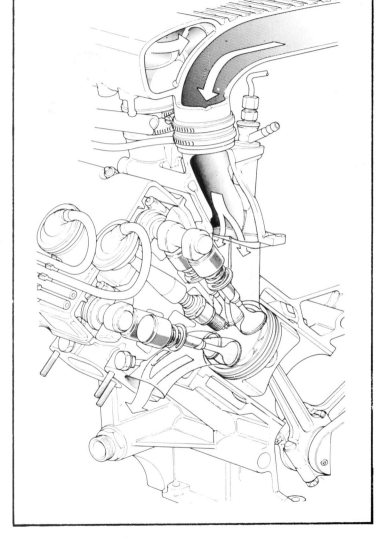

The 308 Quattrovalvole engine is a snug fit behind the rear cockpit bulkhead, but top-end accessibility is good thanks to the twin pneumatic struts which support the compartment lid in a near-vertical position.

There are subtle differences to the front end of the GTS and the GTB as well as the more obvious variations in the window and roof area. Note, for example, the deeper and more rounded skirt beneath the grille of this GTB version of the 308 QV.

The 308GTBi QV in close-up with the famous horse prancing in the centre of the grille as well as in the Ferrari badge above it. The headlamps flash through the lower light units when the wing-mounted lamps are concealed.

The worst excesses of car manufacturers seeking to meet stringent impact regulations in the US market are happily a thing of the past. This is a 1988 308 QV with US-specification bumpers which, though prominent, do not diminish significantly the graceful appearance of the car.

dry, while that wretched needle was still flickering well above the 'empty' stop.

When the injection engine was installed for the first time in 1981, beneath-the-skin chassis changes were carried out in an effort to make what was basically an ageing design compare more favourably with more sophisticated machines such as the Lotus Esprit. The Michelin XWXs gave way to Michelin TRX 205/55VR-390 radials, smaller in overall diameter, but with a fatter section. This necessitated a slight change in ride height, revisions of spring rates and changes to the inner body in order to accommodate those bigger covers when approaching full lock.

The car now displayed a touch of roll, which felt quite reassuring, but I personally felt that the QV displayed a shade too much understeer and the steering was too low-geared for much in the way of extrovert antics on tight country lanes. But an early morning romp with this Ferrari across Salisbury Plain, just after dawn one January morning in 1983, still sticks in my mind as one of the most enjoyable, uninhibited slices of sheer motoring pleasure that I have ever been privileged to enjoy.

Re-acquainting myself with and mastering the tricky first-to-

The roof spoiler, which became a popular option from the introduction of the QV version of the 308GTBi and GTSi, provides a neat bridge between the buttresses flanking the engine compartment.

A neat cover protects the luggage compartment at the rear of this 308GTSi QV and is opened by means of a full-width zip.

The rear bumper of the 308 QV extends just short of the full width of the bodywork, whereas on later cars the lower part wraps round as far as the rear wheelarches.

second gear-change dogleg, the QV sprinted to 60mph in 6.1sec, while 80mph came up in 10sec and 100mph in 15.8sec. Maximum speeds in the gears were 43mph, 60mph, 86mph and 115mph (first to fourth) with the V8 fluttering against its electronic rev-limiter in all cases. Although we did not see over 137mph during the course of the car's stay with us, *Motor* magazine recorded 154.5mph whilst testing at the Millbrook track.

By then – October 1983 – the latest variation on the GTB theme was priced on the UK market at £26,181, tax paid, with another £946.83p for the air conditioning system, which is really an obligatory rather than optional extra in a high-performance machine with such a confined cockpit. Detail shortcomings made it difficult to draw really fair comparisons with such diverse rivals as the Jaguar XJ-S HE (£20,693), the BMW 635 CSi (£23,995) and the Porsche 911 Carrera Sport (£23,366). The instrumentation and, particularly, the cockpit heating system of the Ferrari – still difficult to regulate and direct – did not match up well to those offered by the top performance models from bigger manufacturers.

In North America, the four-valve head allowed the US-specification GTB/GTS to close the performance gap to its European counterparts, power output on these 'de-toxed' models being 230bhp (10bhp down on the Europeans) while peak torque was virtually the same at 188lb/ft at 5,500rpm. Tested by *Car and Driver*, the GTS ran 0-60mph in 7.4sec, cleared 80mph in 11.5sec and took 18.5sec to reach 100mph. It carried a price tag of $59,500.

Meanwhile, fine-tuning the model range specifically for the Italian market and that punitive 2-litre tax break, the Ferrari engineering staff put its heads together with the KKK turbocharger people (with whom they were already collaborating in some depth on the contemporary 120-degree V6 turbo Grand Prix engines) to produce the 208 Turbo based round a 66.8 × 71mm, 1,991cc version of the 90-degree transverse V8. It was introduced at the 1982 Turin Show. With a modest 0.6 bar boost

Just like the 208GT4 before it, the 208GTB Turbo was a product of the Italian taxation laws which severely penalize cars with engines of more than 2 litres displacement. Introduced at the Turin Show in 1982, it could immediately be differentiated from the 3-litre cars by the additional intakes just forward of the rear wheels and by a supplementary grille between the headlamps.

The Ferrari 208 Turbo engine, featuring a KKK turbocharger and Bosch K-Jetronic fuel injection. The exhaust system is fabricated throughout in stainless steel.

pressure and a compression ratio of 7.0:1, this 'domestic' model ran to a maximum of 7,800rpm, developed 220bhp and had a top speed of 150.4mph. Great care was taken to provide smooth, progressive delivery of power, and the modest boost pressure was settled on to ensure that the 208 would perform consistently and reliably without having to devise a way of packaging an intercooling system to keep charge temperatures under control.

Bosch K-Jetronic mechanical fuel injection was also employed on this model, along with Marelli Digiplex electronic ignition. As far as the efficiency of the single-turbo engine was concerned, there was a direct link to contemporary F1 technology with the incorporation of a bypass valve, which recirculated the air back to the turbo through its induction port when the throttle was closed, thereby keeping the turbo spinning so as to ensure prompt response when the throttle was opened again.

Of course, a great deal of care had to be lavished on the exhaust system of this forced-induction engine, so it was manufactured in its entirety out of high-quality stainless steel. Externally, the 208 was distinguished from its naturally aspirated stablemates by the addition of front and rear spoilers, additional air intakes and a supplementary grille on the bonnet.

Introduced at the Frankfurt Show in 1985, the 328 series, with larger-bore and longer-stroke 3.2-litre engine, coincided with more exterior changes including neater wheels and the replacement of separate air vents behind the headlamp pods by a single central extractor grille between them.

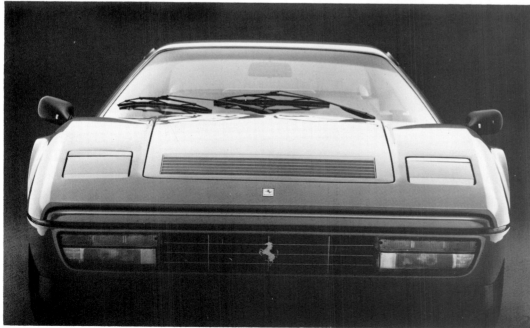

The 328 also brought with it changes to the lighting arrangement at the front. Slimmer units are neatly integrated into a much smoother bumper design on this 328GTB.

Although still officially listed as an optional extra, the roof spoiler above the engine bay has become an increasingly familiar sight since the introduction of the 328 series.

The tail-end treatment was also cleaned up for the introduction of the 328, and as at the front of the car, the lower part of the bumper extends as far as the wheel-arches.

This interior picture of a 328GTB reveals the increasing level of luxury being provided in the eight-cylinder Ferraris. Interestingly, all instruments are back on the facia, the centre console once again being used for controls only.

Turbo technology was one area where Ferrari was accumulating know-how at a tremendous pace, via its racing programme, and with increased data on the problems of heat dissipation in turbocharged engines coming to hand all the time, it was not surprising that the 208 benefited from this input. By 1986, a Behr intercooler had been added to the engine's specification, ceramic-coated cylinder liners and other subtle improvements allowing the boost pressure to be increased to 1.05bar with no loss of reliability.

A Japanese IHI turbocharger now replaced the KKK unit, power output being raised from 220bhp to 254bhp at 6500rpm and torque to 242.3lb/ft at 4,100rpm. The 208 would now top 157mph.

As far as the 'mainstream' development of the Dino 308 lineage was concerned, the continuous process of development manifested itself in the arrival of the 328 which was launched at the 1985 Frankfurt Show. Including a GTB, GTS, Mondial and Mondial Cabriolet, as before, Ferrari's 'volume' range was now powered by the latest variant of that long-lived 90-degree transverse V8.

With a bore and stroke of 83 × 73mm, the 3,195cc unit pushed out 270bhp at 7,000rpm with 223lb/ft of torque. The engine retained its alloy crankcase, but now had shrunken-in liners made out of aluminium, replacing the cast-iron liners on the injected QV range. Marelli Microplex electronic ignition with static advance was employed, while fuel injection remained the familiar and reliable Bosch K-Jetronic mechanical system.

The braking system on the 328 remained substantially unchanged, although the adoption of Mondial 8 calipers offered more pad area, and the handbrake now worked on small rear supplementary drums and was more effective than the 308's.

The Ferrari 328GTS, this time without a roof spoiler, but with just the chin and tail spoilers augmenting the subtle lip which is integrated into the rear of the bodywork. This low-angle view reveals a useful amount of ground clearance beneath the unladen car.

Interior trim was generally unchanged, but the instrumentation had been subtly improved, now being identical to that in the 288GTO, Maranello's splendid Group B supercar, which is dealt with in a later chapter.

The door handles, interior pockets and armrests were re-designed on this model, while the controls for the heating/demisting systems were now colour-coded and touch-sensitive, and were positioned between the seats, where they replaced the sliding-bar system which had become so familiar to many customers over the years. Whether this was a step in the right direction, or merely change for change's sake, remained a matter for debate.

The front and rear bumpers were now colour-matched with the rest of the car, the alloy wheels were restyled, and the cooling vents on the top of the front wheelarches were replaced by additional venting in the centre of the bonnet section, between the retractable headlights. The light clusters either side of the main grille were new.

The chin spoiler beneath the nose, previously an extra, now came as standard equipment, while a spoiler across the engine bay just behind the rear window was optional, as was metallic paint (£599.25p in the UK), air conditioning (£1,499.99p) and number plates (£20). The 328 came with Goodyear NCTs as original equipment, 205/55VR-16 (front) and 225/50VR-16 (rear), rim widths being 7 and 8in respectively.

(The adoption of Goodyear tyres as standard equipment in place of Michelins was one of the by-products of the Ferrari F1 team's switch from the French radials back to Akron products at the start of the 1982 season.)

As far as performance was concerned, the 328GTB more than

Convex-shaped wheels adorned the Mondial 3.2 on its introduction in 1985. As with the GTB and GTS models, there were a number of minor styling changes, especially at the front of the car.

Marketed as the 3.2 Mondial Cabriolet, the latest open-topped car in the series displays a particularly neat integration of bumpers and bodywork, but as this side view makes clear, it has not been possible to disguise the fact that the substantial top takes up a lot of space behind the seats.

sustained the pace of its opposition, sprinting from 0-60mph in a shade less than 6sec and reaching 100mph in 14.7sec, by which time it was pulling lustily in fourth gear.

It represented, in many ways, Ferrari's technical triumph over the vagaries of emission control regulations. That switch from carburettors to fuel injection on the original two-valves-per-cylinder GTB, at the turn of the decade, had rendered the prancing horse slightly lame. With first the QV and then the 328, Ferrari had overcome the challenge to reassert the GTB's market position as a stunning off-the-peg supercar.

The instrument and control layouts of the Mondial and the GTB/GTS models are very different. The Mondial 3.2, pictured on the previous page, retains the horizontal theme for the instrument panel while the audio equipment is built into the front end of the centre console. In contrast, the car on the right (a 208GTB Turbo) has a much more packed facia and a thin stem extending forwards from the shorter console to the front cockpit bulkhead. Note also the different design of steering wheels.

This is what you see in your rear-view mirror when a 3.2 Mondial rushes up behind you. Unlike the GTB/GTS models, the Mondial has an air vent running the full width of the panel behind the headlamp covers, the latter being considerably wider in this case to house dual light units. Indicator repeater lights are forward of the front wheels whereas on the GTB and GTS they are behind them.

Inevitably, GTBs and GTSs are prime targets for car converters and performance enhancers, although not always with aesthetic success. This is a 328GTS after the attention of Koenig of Munich, an elaborate conversion involving a deep front airdam, flared wheelarches, additional side air intakes and a racing-type rear wing. Hidden is the turbocharger, which is said to boost output to 450bhp.

CHAPTER 9

What to look for

Buying and running a small Ferrari

If you are looking for a secondhand high-performance car to drive, park in your garage, switch off and walk away – then expect to return a week or so later, switch on and drive away without any fuss – don't even consider a used Ferrari. These may sound like harsh words, but they are the facts of the matter. Owning a Ferrari is like having an affair; it takes a great deal of effort and energy, can be nerve-wracking, time-consuming and supremely irritating. But, for the true enthusiast, the joy derived from 'making it all work' transcends all the negative aspects.

The other golden rule to bear in mind is that old adage 'you get what you pay for'. It applies to buying secondhand Ferraris more than most used cars. Although Ferrari has moved into the computer age over the last few years, and is now making cars of a quality that is remarkable by its standards 10-15 years ago, this progress is only relatively recent. Moreover, for all this progress, the modern Ferrari is a complex piece of machinery which should be treated with kid gloves from the very start of its life. Abuse a Ferrari and you will surely reap a whirlwind of bills! The trick is, of course, to ensure that *you* do not wind up collecting the tab for the lack of thought and mechanical consideration of others.

In the case of the Dino 246, it is now over 14 years since the last of these delectable machines rolled off the Maranello production lines. At that time the Italian motor industry was not exactly renowned for the quality of steel it employed. There is no question at all that, correctly prepared and tuned, with plenty of loving care lavished on it, a 15-years-old Dino 246 can still be an absolute joy to drive. But should you choose to acquire a badly neglected, abused or 'tarted up' example, be prepared to write cheques *ad infinitum*.

A rusty, badly neglected Dino can be a nightmare, so it is worth seeking specialist advice before you set out on the trail of a possible purchase. There are many reputable Ferrari specialists – in addition to importers Maranello Concessionaries – who will be prepared to look over an individual car and give you an objective assessment of its condition and potential for restoration. Money invested in this way at the start of a project will almost certainly repay itself several times over later in the car's life.

The most obvious thing to look for if you are trying to assess a car on your own is its service history. If the previous owner does not have a fairly accurate record of what's been done when, then the warning lights should flash. Unless you have a particularly well-equipped workshop and, indeed, are more than just an amateur 'tinkerer', it is not advisable to get involved in home maintenance. The 246 has an extremely rigorous service schedule. For example, Modena Engineering, the East Horsley-based specialists who have enormous experience of working with these cars, require a minimum of three days to complete a full service on a 246.

Corrosion damage is obviously another area to watch carefully. The key places to check are around all four wheelarches, at the bottom of the front and rear wings, the sills and along the bottom of the doors themselves. It is important to bear in mind that, when the cars were new, the rearward section of the front wing, at the point where it faces the leading edge of the door, was a double-skinned section, as was a large area of the structure around the rear wheelarches. Should you find an example which, strangely, appears to be single-skinned around this section, it is best to walk away. The tin worm has almost certainly been at work with a vengeance and the car cobbled up.

Remember that the people who bought Dino 246s in their early days were probably new to the Ferrari range, probably switching from Porsche or other specialist sports cars with a better overall reliability record that the machines from Maranello. As a direct consequence of this, it is likely than many original owners were less atuned to the fact that their new car needed more frequent specialist attention than they had been accustomed to giving their previous machines. It's not necessarily that they were lacking in discernment; many were simply not aware of the nature of the beast they were acquiring. Consequently, the 246 is beset by more problems resulting from straightforward neglect than most elderly Ferraris.

The anti-corrosion protection of the early Dinos was not of a high order. The front wings, sills and doors received the bare minimum of protection and, should you find yourself in the position of having to take the entire bodyshell off for a ground-up restoration, you will almost certainly find that new sills will be necessary in addition to replacing the outriggers on which the bodyshell is mounted.

Alloy was used for the outer skins of the front bonnet panel, the engine cover and rear luggage hatch, but the remainder of the car was manufactured from rust-prone steel – in contrast to the earlier 206GT, which had an all-aluminium bodyshell. A wary eye should be kept open for deterioration on the edge of the fins which extend backwards from the roofline down to the rear wings.

The Dino 246 floorpan and undertray are made from glass-fibre, the latter attached to the chassis tubes and outer sills by means of pop-rivets. Inevitably, with the passage of time, these rivets fracture, with the danger that the undertray may drop down on to the road. Be certain that the undertray is in place on any car you may be considering because one of its functions is to keep dirt, grime and road spray away from the rust-vulnerable cross-tubes which brace the chassis structure.

One of the specialists I spoke to described the Dino 246 as 'what amounts to an up-market Mini-Cooper S. It lacked sheer grunt, so to make it move quickly one was forever racing up and down through the gears, making the engine rev its head off!'

That may sound like heresay to a Ferrari fan, but it certainly highlights the way in which many Dinos were used by their original owners. The net result was a high level of engine wear. Many Dino 246s were well-worn within a very short lifespan.

To put it bluntly, the Dino 246 camshafts are bad news; they are very susceptible to wear and there is the possibility of actually knocking off a lobe if the valve clearances are not kept to their optimum adjustment. Unfortunately, the rather inaccessible engine installation makes this a complex and time-consuming task; many owners tend to overlook it. You must consider that it will take a day's hard work to adjust the valves and that this is a job that must be done every 6,000 miles if the engine is to be kept in top trim.

The chains which drive the camshaft are also very susceptible to wear and the core plugs are prone to leaking in the iron block. The oil pressure sender often develops a fault, sending inaccurate signals to the oil pressure gauge, thereby wrongly indicating that the engine has a lubricant problem.

The gearbox is vulnerable to misuse. One of the biggest problems that an owner can encounter is when the synchromesh on second gear packs up, the legacy of sustained heavy loadings. To replace a faulty synchro assembly involves removing the entire engine/gearbox package and it can take as much as a week's intensive work if the opportunity is taken to rebuild the gearbox at the same time.

Oil circulation has always been something of a marginal area on the Dino V6, so one should always take care to warm up the car very gently indeed for the first two or three minutes after starting from cold. Owners have not always understood the necessity for regular oil changes on these cars, with the result that bearing wear has been hastened and more expensive problems have arisen.

Electrics generally are suspect. Some owners have replaced the unreliable Marelli Dinoplex electronic ignition system with a more modern Bosch system in order to get over the general unreliability of the original equipment, and another occasional complaint has been of alternator overcharging caused by the regulator being wired incorrectly.

Moving up to the Bertone-styled 308GT4, it is as well to remember that this model went through a phase of being the unloved ugly duckling of the Ferrari range after its replacement by the more graceful Pininfarina-styled 308. Partly as a result of this, the first V8-engined Dinos found themselves falling into the hands of unsympathetic owners as their value plummeted, with

Proper restoration is a time-consuming and often expensive business, and due allowance for it should be made before deciding how much to pay for a used car. This Dino 246GT has been stripped right back to the bare metal, a wise precaution with a model which was always rust-prone.

the consequent risk of further neglect and deterioration.

Until the mid-1980s, the GT4 represented outstanding value for the Ferrari buyer, but now the cars have become rather more appreciated amongst the discerning enthusiasts, with the result that their prices have hardened somewhat. But the same basic constraints apply to this bigger Dino as her older sister; buy cheap, buy twice...

The wet-sump four-cam V8 is basically a tough, durable engine, but that fact does not mean the owner should take it for granted or ignore the basic ground rules of cosseting any Ferrari of any age.

Most of the common V8 engine ailments are caused by constant revving when cold. Watch for excessive piston ring wear, as evidenced by the blowing of too much blue smoke. Bear in mind that the toothed rubber belt driving the camshafts should be replaced at an absolute maximum of 30,000-mile intervals, possibly even as early as 24,000 miles; specialist advice varies between these two norms. However, providing it is serviced properly, and the tappets, carburettors and ignition are kept in tune, it is a sturdy piece of engineering.

Keep an eye out for oil leakage, and pay careful attention to see that the head gaskets are not leaking. There are two quite straight-forward methods of checking this. First, remove the dipstick and examine a trace of oil; if it shows signs of thinning, this could be because water is seeping into the sump. Secondly, under normal conditions, the water temperature should rise to its optimum level within a few minutes of firing up the engine. If it does not, this could be the first sign of trouble.

As on the Dino 246, second gear is the ratio most prone to problems, and a test drive for more than a few miles is really the

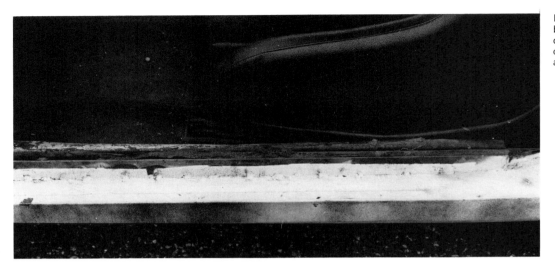

Door sills are amongst the first places to be examined when assessing the condition of bodywork. In this case, badly corroded metal will have to be cut out and replaced.

only way in which any potential trouble in this area can be assessed. When cold, avoid using second by changing from first to third until the 'box is properly warmed up. Then it should be quite possible to slip the gear in without any baulking at all. If it refuses to select smoothly and cleanly, then think again. This could well signal an impending problem with the synchromesh.

A check for body corrosion is also a major priority. Open the bonnet and boot and check round the inside edges for any bubbling or first signs of deterioration. Moisture tends to accumulate in the rear wheelarches and lower quarter panels, while the drain plugs at the bottom of the doors also trap water, with resultant severe corrosion to the bottom panel and outer skin. The inner and outer sills are made from unexpectedly thin-gauge metal, so check round this area. The front wings are also a danger spot.

Take the trouble to cast a critical eye over the GT4's suspension components. Check for worn ball-joints and try to ascertain whether or not the system has received regular greasing. The handbrake requires regular adjustment, and neglect can also result in badly scored brake discs, which can be expensive to replace.

Clutches and water pumps can be troublesome. Look carefully to see that the heat shields on the exhaust manifold have not rusted through and do the same for the exhaust system. This does not enjoy a long life and is very costly to replace. The fuse box is also a problem area, tending towards overheating and blowing fuses as a result, while the GT4 shares the same problem as the 246 in that the oil sender unit can go on the blink and produce inaccurate instrument readings.

As far as the 308GTB is concerned, it is supremely ironic that the original glass-fibre-bodied cars are now regarded as the ultimate collector's item and are in the shortest supply. Their arrival on the US market was greeted with wariness by potential purchasers, apprehensive of such an *avant garde* approach from a manufacturer who had always previously stuck with steel-bodied cars. The factory originally anticipated it would be able to make these 308s not only lighter – which it did, to the tune of 250lb saved – but also at a lower cost. However, when production settled down it soon became clear that Scaglietti simply could not produce the glass-fibre-bodied cars quickly enough and, at the time the first spider model was introduced, the factory made a complete change, almost overnight, to the steel-bodied cars.

Records indicate that less than 80 of these glass-fibre-bodied machines found their way into the UK and, although prices on such collectables are changing virtually day by day, in February 1988, expert opinion priced such a 308 at over £30,000.

Bearing in mind that these glass-fibre-bodied GTBs have been recognized as collectors' pieces for several years, any example now coming onto the secondhand market will have been treated with a fair degree of care, so it will be the condition of engine, transmission and other running gear that should be examined as a major priority. Remember, of course, that even the glass-fibre-bodied cars had steel sills, which should be examined for signs of deterioration and rust, but the paintwork was of a lustrous and high quality.

General points to keep in mind for all 308s are the state of the wishbone bushes, which tend to wear pretty quickly, and any potential purchaser should keep their ear open for slight mechanical 'clunks' from the rear end, indicating that the shock absorber bushes are beginning to wear.

By the late 1970s, the V8 engine had developed a pretty high standard of reliability, assuming it was serviced correctly, but the same tell-tale signs of wear and tear – smoking exhausts and chattering camshafts – should be watched for, as on the GT4. But as long as they are kept in tune, the general feeling is that Fiat's influence gradually rubbed off in making the engines more easily maintainable through the evolution of the fuel-injected and Quattrovalvole variations.

The ravages of time have inevitably caught up with many of the earlier steel-bodied 308s, especially those made before 1983/84, when Maranello began a serious anti-corrosion programme.

The low-grade steel used by most Italian car makers in the

The engine bay of the Dino 246GT. Removal of the engine is another time-consuming task, but often essential during the restoration process. Even top-end work on the power unit should not be tackled without first removing the compartment cover.

An immaculate Dino 246GT awaiting its next owner. This is one of the world's most desirable cars, but ownership implies a responsibility to ensure that all the hard work which has been put into it will not go to waste through neglect.

However immaculate a used Ferrari may appear, remember that it could well have endured a hard life. These skid marks on the pit road at Donington bear witness not only to an expensive layer of rubber from this 308GTB QV but also to a hard-worked clutch. Fun in Ferraris rarely comes cheaply!

mid-1970s ensured that any early steel-bodied 308 not maintained to the most stringent standards is likely to have deteriorated quite badly.

Check for poor resprays on the glass-fibre-bodied versions, as well as doors which should shut with a perfect fit, almost as if they were steel. On the steel-bodied cars, watch for insidious rust round the front wings – always a problem area – but the doors are definitely less prone to deterioration than on the GT4, providing the drain holes have been kept clear. In fact, there are a lot of cleverly-sited drain holes on the GTBs, including two at the front end of the bonnet.

Home servicing is not recommended, and is not the work of a moment. For example, to change the plugs on the 'leading' bank of the transverse-mounted V8, it is almost essential to remove the hinged engine cover completely. As a result, the less scrupulous dealers may 'forget' to carry out this task during routine servicing, so it is always worth insisting on a bill which specifically itemizes all the work that has been carried out. The electrical system is nothing for Ferrari to be proud of and minor failures must be expected, although the Veglia instrumentation is generally pretty reliable.

As far as servicing is concerned, Maranello Concessionaries, the highly regarded UK importers based at Egham, in Surrey, scores highly with all the specialists we consulted, and although they are expensive, their reputation for fair dealing, high standards of service and dependability was echoed by many of the unofficial, but respected, Ferrari specialists who do not benefit from affiliation with the factory. A list of some of the more prominent specialists is included later in this section, some familiar to all Ferrari enthusiasts, others perhaps less well-known, who have made names for themselves relatively recently.

If one is considering the purchase of a relatively recent GTB, say since the advent of the QV range, then a service history provides a good pointer to the amount of attention (or otherwise) that may have been lavished on it. But it is of paramount importance to remember that you are *not* dealing with a run-of-the-mill motor car when buying any of the models mentioned in this book. There is absolutely no point at all in attempting to cut corners, nor can one expect to find, for example, a wide selection of 15-year-old 246s with religiously-logged maintenance records from Maranello Concessionaries.

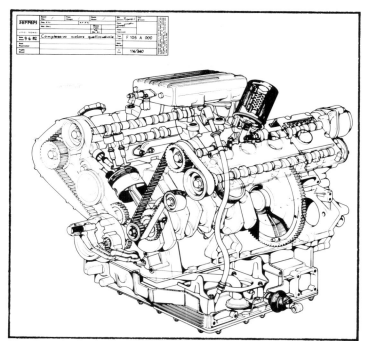

The Ferrari V8 engine in its 3-litre Quattrovalvole form is generally considered to be a robust power unit, but like nearly all high-performance engines it does not take kindly to abuse, especially when cold. A comprehensive maintenance log is often a reliable guide to previous ownership in sympathetic hands.

Ultimately, a certain degree of seat-of-pants judgment must be exercised in acquiring any Ferrari more than three or four years old, so inevitably, reliance on specialist attention is to be recommended. Unless you are contemplating buying from an established official dealer, commissioning a specialist engineer to carry out a detailed examination may be a wise investment. On the face of it, the expenditure of £300 to £400 may seem a lot, but weighed against the cost of a car in the £30,000 bracket it is certainly a drop in the ocean – not to mention what it could save in terms of restoration and repair if you spend the money and then find that considerable additional outlay is required getting the car up to standard.

An alternative way of buying a used Ferrari is offered by an organization called SuperCar, one of the partners in which is racing driver David Hunt, younger brother of 1976 World Champion James. Supercar operates as an agency, matching potential buyers with sellers and taking a commission from each. They can also act as principal in such a deal, if required, and claim that the major advantage with the service they offer is an ability to be totally objective in their assessment of any car they might be asked to examine.

Although it is possible for SuperCar to locate and arrange the purchase of used Ferraris to a very specific and defined specification, Hunt says that most of their customers commission his organization with quite a wide brief when it comes to looking for any particular model. Once a suitable car has been tracked down, they can either opt for David or his partner to inspect it – 'after a time you develop an intuitive knowledge as to whether a Ferrari has been cared for or abused' – or get a full engineer's report carried out. Although accident damage is one pointer to condition, David is adamant that this should not, in itself, put one off buying a Ferrari. If it has been repaired properly by a reputable

The compartments for the swivelling headlamps are notorious for attracting corrosion on some models and are always worth a close inspection before purchase and at regular intervals afterwards.

Be prepared to examine a Ferrari at ground level. A seemingly immaculate car can reveal a grisly picture underneath. The day after this picture was taken this 308GT4 was in the bodyshop for some substantial work on the sills.

A potential trouble area is the vertical face at the rear of the front wing, which, even when the door is open, remains partly obscured. Careful examination is highly recommended.

Take a close look, too, at the exhaust system and to the body panelling adjacent to it, which, being relatively inaccessible, is often overlooked during routine cleaning and polishing, with dire consequences.

company, it should be up to scratch, in his view. He also makes the point that, with prices showing steady growth, even a late-1970s 308 is becoming regarded as a classic, historic car, with the result that an increasing number have been restored and a greater percentage have been previously owned by caring and sympathetic enthusiasts. However, there will always be a number of buyers who feel that 'they know best' and will attempt to run one of these Ferraris as economically as possible. Their cars are generally the ones to avoid.

Component prices vary quite considerably, depending on sources, but as a 1988 index of the sort of cost ownership of the cars mentioned in this volume will involve, a windscreen for a 308 will set you back between £320 and £340; a clutch for a Dino 246 is between £160 and £180; one of the four camshafts for the same is £120; and a rear bumper for a 308GT4 is £220. The message is to shop around, but also to be sufficiently well-informed about what you are trying to obtain to know whether or not you have actually received the right component, rather than a very similar one from another model. From what the author has heard, there are one or two pleasantly chaotic, if extremely willing, dealers in the business who don't seem to be totally sure themselves about precise component specifications!

To sum up, I would quote my good friend Terry Hoyle, whose specialist engine-rebuilding base at Maldon, in Essex, has gained a highly regarded reputation for building just about every sort of power plant from rally Audi Quattros, through racing Sierra Cosworths to Ferrari 275GTBs and Lussos:

' I believe that, properly maintained, a Ferrari will run forever. But it is no use thinking that you are dealing with an old Granada, which you can just drive, drive and drive until it is run into the ground. Neglect a Ferrari and it will wear out extremely quickly; service it properly, tend it, care for it and always carry out routine maintenance when it is required, rather than when you think you have time to do so, and it will last as long as you want it to!'

Where to look

It was back in Mike Hawthorn's day that Colonel Ronnie Hoare began importing Ferraris into the UK, so any search for a decent used model should include Maranello Concessionaries, whose technical base is at Thorpe Industrial Estate, Ten Acre Lane, Thorpe, Egham, Surrey (0784 36222), while Maranello Sales, Egham By-Pass (A30), Egham, Surrey (0784 36431) can show you a representative selection of used Ferraris, many of which were probably supplied by the same organization to their original owners.

Other official Ferrari dealers in the UK are H. R. Owen, in London (01-998 7691); Reg Vardy, in Tyne and Wear (0783 842842); Stanley Harvey, in Belfast (0232 232111); Lancaster Garages, in Colchester (0206 48141); H. A. Fox, in Torquay (0303 24321); Colmore Car People, in West Bromwich (021 553 7500); Emblem Sports Cars (UK), in Blandford (0258 51211);

JCT 600, in Bradford (0274 392321); Melbourne Garage, in Jersey (0534 62709); Brandon Motors, near Coventry (0203 542285); Strattons, of Wilmslow (0625 532678) and Glen Henderson, in Ayr (0292 281531).

The ever-helpful Ken Bradshaw, at the Ferrari Owners' Club (0676 34862), will probably be in a position to give some pointers on where to look for good specialist services, but any potential Ferrari owner would be well advised to join the FOC anyway. For a modest annual subscription there is an attractive quarterly magazine, a bi-monthly newsletter, plenty of social activity, plus the opportunity to participate in sprints, hillclimbs and races, including the well-supported Maranello Michelin Challenge, now in its third year, which brings out of hiding plenty of enthusiastic owners quite prepared to risk their 308s, etc, in wheel-to-wheel track confrontation. Don't put Ken or the club on the spot, though, by asking for any specific recommendations about individual firms; however, it doesn't take you much time in the presence of Ferrari folk to get quite an accurate feel for companies that do a good job.

In the course of my investigations, several names came up again and again. In no particular order, they are Modena Engineering, Station Garage, Ockham Road South, East Horsley, Surrey (04865 4663); Graypaul Motors, Halstead Road, Mountsorrel, New Loughborough, Leicestershire (0533 374051); DK Engineering, Unit D, 200 Rickmansworth Road, Watford, Herts (0923 55246); Terry Hoyle, Unit 6, Heybridge House Industrial Estate, Maldon, Essex (0621 55391); Euro Spares, 8 Rosemary Lane, Halstead, Essex (0787 473678); Fullbridge Carriage Company, Fullbridge Wharf, Maldon, Essex (0621 52320).

CHAPTER 10

288GTO and F40

Blood brothers

The supercars that Ferrari put into limited production in the mid-1980s are not strictly part of the 308/328 lineage, though they have a family resemblance, use the same basic V8 engine and share a number of other fundamental parts with the mainstream cars.

Both the 1984 288GTO and the 1987 F40 were destined to become 'instant classics', combining shattering performance with rare exclusivity. They are, 12-cylinder Daytonas, Boxers and Testarossas notwithstanding, the most powerful roadgoing Ferraris ever built.

When the 288GTO was launched in 1984, it was 20 years since the heyday of the magnificent front-engined 250GTO that won three GT racing World Championships. Manufacturers of high-performance cars were faced with many more regulations and restrictions than they had been two decades earlier. A new GTO, whether or not it was to go racing, would have to be a very different kind of car if some were to be released for road use.

It is generally supposed that Ferrari did have racing in mind when the 288GTO was planned, and the projected production of 200 cars suggests that they were aiming for Group B homologation. Porsche had similar plans with the car that became the 959, and the adoption of Group B as an important category seemed on the cards.

This didn't happen, and so Ferrari, like Porsche, went ahead with their limited edition of super-powerful, super-expensive cars as a prestige venture to promote the technical excellence and ingenuity of the marque.

The 288 certainly lived up to this role. The body has a clear similarity to the GTB, but underneath, the V8 engine, of 2,855cc and turbocharged to give no less than 400bhp, is mounted longitudinally, racing style, with the gearbox behind it.

In this form, the 32-valve V8 has bore and stroke dimensions of 80×71mm. The light-alloy block has aluminium liners with a special chemical nickel coating (Nikasil). With a compression ratio of 7.6:1, the GTO has two Japanese IHI turbochargers set to a maximum boost of 11.6psi (0.8 bar). Charge air is cooled by two Behr heat exchangers mounted above and just to the back of the engine. The resulting output is quoted at 400bhp at 7,000rpm with 366lb/ft of torque at 3,800rpm.

Drawing from the Ferrari Formula 1 team's experience, the 288 utilizes Weber-Marelli IAW electronic injection and ignition. This comprises two complete sets of equipment, one for each bank of cylinders.

The specially-designed five-speed gearbox and transaxle, incorporating a limited-slip differential, also drew heavily on F1 technology. The clutch is an 8.5in diameter twin-plate type, hydraulically controlled and identical to that of the Grand Prix cars.

The suspension layout is similar to the 308's – double wishbones front and rear, though tubular and made from special steel. Ventilated disc brakes are fitted all round, and a servo is provided.

The GTO's body, designed as ever in collaboration with Pininfarina, is Ferrari's first road car application of F1 composite-materials technology. Though most of the body is glass-fibre, Kevlar, Nomex and aluminium honeycomb are all in use, with carbon-fibre for stiffening in key areas. The 288GTO's kerb weight is 2,557lb.

Flared front wings, larger auxiliary driving lights and a comprehensive display of air intakes and extractor vents contribute to the impressive front end of the 288GTO, an exciting high-performance interpretation of the GTB theme.

Factory performance figures give the GTO's maximum speed as 189mph and 0-100mph acceleration in 11sec. It can pull over 100mph in second gear and 150mph in third. No forgiving, muted performance road car, this, but a thinly-veiled street racer.

The GTO even had some of the world's top Grand Prix drivers queueing to put their money down. Formula 1 folklore had it that only 200 would be made until Niki Lauda, twice World Champion for Ferrari, came along with his order. That would be the 201st, and last, they said. But at an ex-works price of around £80,000, the GTO was not as outrageous as the Porsche 959 and it attracted more customers with money in hand than Ferrari expected. In the end they made 272.

Quite a number were sold for an immediate profit, at up to £20,000 premium. Many were tucked away in heated motor houses to further appreciate in value. Not many were used as everyday transport, but some of the Grand Prix drivers drove theirs on the road – before they sold them! Eddie Cheever, for one, eulogized about one particular run down the *autostrada* from Milan to Rome, then back on secondary roads. By the end of that trip, Cheever's GTO was panting like a dog with its tongue hanging out. 'A real road racer', he enthused. Incidentally, Cheever's wife Rita refused to ride with him in it...

When GTO production was concluded, there seems to have been a realization at Maranello that they could have extracted more out of this very special car. Though the prototype of an 'evolution' racing version was produced, the 288 was not destined for competition. Clearly there were customers for such expensive cars, more than they realized. Perhaps they should repeat the idea, with an even more sophisticated car, even closer to racing, and charge considerably more for it?

The 288GTO is rarely seen from this angle, which is a pity because it identifies clearly the areas of both similarity and difference compared with Pininfarina's design for the GTB.

The 288GTO was the focal point of interest on the Ferrari stand when it made its debut at the 1984 Geneva Show. Only 200 examples were expected to be made, but in fact 272 cars eventually left the factory.

Unlike the cars in the 308/328 series, the GTO's V8 engine is mounted longitudinally ahead of its five-speed transmission, which means that the engine cover extends well into the usual cockpit area. In this picture the engine is dwarfed by the twin intercoolers and by the complex exhaust system beneath the turbo wastegate.

The businesslike instrument and control layout of the GTO has much in common with that of the later GTB/GTS models. Note the matt-finished trim for the entire facia area, the carpeting on the walls of the footwell and the large rest provided to the left of the clutch pedal.

Misinterpreted pictures of mystery Ferraris seen around the works suggested a four-wheel-drive 959 competitor, and there were rumours of a new LM, recalling Ferrari's last Le Mans winner. The four-wheel-drive car turned out to be an experimental prototype, unrelated to the next supercar. LM was nearly right, for as Enzo Ferrari said in July 1987: 'On June 6, 1986 I expressed the wish to our executive committee to have a car reminiscent of the original 250LM'. Just 12 months later he presented the result. The type, it was decided just before announcement, would be F40, commemorating the 40th anniversary of the first car to carry the Ferrari name.

It was rolled out on to the Fiorano test track – and lapped quicker than the late Gilles Villeneuve ever managed in a 1980 3-litre 312T5 Formula 1 car.

Even without its identification on the rear panel, this car would be recognizable as a GTO by its flared arches with cooling vents behind the rear wheels and by the conspicuous endplate to the five-speed gearbox.

Ferrari's next venture into the realm of ultra-high-performance road cars was the F40, which was introduced in 1987 to mark the 40th anniversary of the first car to carry the Ferrari name.

Embodying competition car body technology, the F40 makes wide use of carbon-fibre and composite structural materials, although like the GTO, its chassis is based on a tubular-steel frame to which the body panels are bonded.

The impressive power source for the F40, a 2,963cc V8 engine with twin IHI turbochargers running at up to 1.1 bar and Marelli/Weber electronic fuel injection and ignition, delivers 478bhp and 425lb/ft of torque, sufficient to give the car a top speed in excess of 200mph.

The view most people are likely to see of an F40 — going away from them rapidly. Extractor vents in the rear screen, on the top of the rear deck beneath the massive wing and behind the rear wheels testify to the potential heat build-up from such a potent package.

The interior of the F40 is deliberately spartan, but contains neatly recessed instruments, convenient controls and well-padded and carefully moulded lightweight seats. A racing car for the road, if ever there was.

By the time the F40 was revealed it was almost too late to order one. Ferrari had already received blank-cheque orders from a few hundred of their regular customers who can't help themselves when it comes to Maranello exotica.

In the UK, the price was estimated at £160,000. Compared to the 288GTO, the F40's production looked generous from the outset. A total of 450 were scheduled for build, running to the end of 1989.

Ferrari engineers admitted that the F40 was essentially the GTO *Evoluzione* refined for limited production. It was intended to extend the use of Formula 1 technology – composite materials, aerodynamics and turbocharged engine – to a practical road car.

The body makes considerably more use of carbon-fibre and composite structural materials than the GTO's. It remains based on a tubular-steel frame and the body panels are bonded to that with a specially developed adhesive. Ferrari claim that the production technique has only previously been used for competition cars.

The chassis layout remains similar to the GTO, but the engine has a massive increase in power. It is a 2,963cc, 82 × 69.5mm

In wet weather, the doors should be continuously washed by tyre spray. The large extractor ducts have an aerodynamic function as well as aiding heat dissipation.

Twin intercoolers dominate the top of the engine compartment of the F40, which is braced by a large-diameter tubular-steel strut. The entire rear end of the car is exposed by lifting the one-piece roof-hinged cover.

version of the V8, again using two IHI turbos and Marelli/Weber electronic injection and ignition. Boost is set at 1.1 bar, maximum power is 478bhp at 7,000rpm, and torque is 425lb/ft at 4,000rpm.

With a kerb weight of 2,650lb, the factory claimed a maximum speed above the magic 200mph – 201mph to be precise – and a standing-kilometre time of 21sec. As this is written, a production car has yet to be seen, and no independent testers have been able to take performance figures.

What is clear from its carefully detailed aerodynamically tuned bodywork, its stark interior (no soft trim, sliding side windows), and the provision of proper foam-filled fuel tanks as well as options such as a transmission with straight-cut gears, is that the F40 is very nearly a ready-to-go racer. But there are few signs that anyone will use it as such. It remains, for now, the ultimate in Ferrari road performance. And it owes its origins to the Dino series.

You simply pull the communication cord when wishing to make contact with the outside world, unless of course you prefer to shout through the opening of the F40's sliding door window.

The ins and outs of airflow around the rear of the F40. The initial schedule for 450 of these cars to be built by the end of 1989 was subsequently doubled in response to heavy demand.

Although conceived by the IDEA styling institute in Turin as a proposed PPG pace car for Indy Car racing in the United States, this smoothly contoured prototype would now seem destined for a much more significant role. A development of it is expected to become the Mondial replacement in 1990.

Certainly the IDEA car's longitudinal engine placement has been adopted for the next generation of V8-engined Ferrari road cars. The horizontal ribs which dominate the rear end of this design are a reminder of the Mercedes-Benz C111 Wankel rotary-engined experimental cars of the early 1970s. Unlike the German cars, however, this Ferrari does point the way towards production models of the future.

CHAPTER 11

The Fiat Dinos

Second cousins

Enzo Ferrari had always seen road car production as a way of financing his first love, motor racing, and with the Fiat Dino collaboration he killed a couple of birds with one well-aimed stone.

He got the engine he required to enter Formula 2 racing under the new rules that came into force in 1967 and one which would form the basis of a new kind of Ferrari road car. Fiat were keen to maintain close links with the marque that had done so much for Italy's prestige abroad. Both parties were to enter into an arrangement which would show the benefits of an altogether more intimate relationship.

As detailed elsewhere, the marriage took place in June 1969. The Fiat model that would allow the Dino V6 engine to be made in suitable numbers to meet the F2 rules had been revealed three years earlier at the Turin Show. Their idea was to have a sporting flagship for the Fiat range, replacing the 2300S coupe. There were to be two distinct Fiat Dino models: a Bertone-bodied 2 + 2 coupe and a Pininfarina open two-seater spider.

They used a detuned version of the V6 designed by Franco Rocchi and developed for production by Fiat's Aurelio Lampredi – who had left Ferrari in 1955. Initially aluminium-cased with the dimensions 86 × 57mm, 1,987cc, it developed 160bhp at 7,200rpm, compared with Ferrari's quoted 180bhp for the Dino 206GT. The difference in power is controversial, for apart from carburettor jets and the exhaust, there was virtually no difference between them – and both types were made by Fiat.

For their Dinos, Fiat mounted the engine conventionally, in-line at the front, and it drove the rear wheels by a live rear axle, via a five-speed all-syncromesh gearbox.

Though different in wheelbase (spider 90in, coupe 100in) the models shared the same mechanical specification. Both models were of unitary construction, the basic floorpans being supplied by Fiat to the coachbuilders – and later returned complete to their Rivalta plant for final assembly.

The Dino's suspension was essentially borrowed from the Fiat 125 saloon. At the rear, it had semi-elliptic single-leaf springs, with radius arms to control axle tramp and two shock absorbers per wheel. Double wishbones with coil springs were used at the front, with an anti-roll bar. Brakes were servo-assisted discs all round. The centre-lock 14in diameter Elektron wheels wore 185/14 Michelin XAS radial-ply tyres.

With a top speed close to 130mph and 0-60mph acceleration in the order of 8sec, these were extraordinary Fiats! And they were very well thought-of, for all the race-bred camshaft clattering of the Ferrari engine.

The late John Bolster, writing in *Autosport* after testing the Dino spider in 1967, described it as 'a driver's car *par excellence*', adding: 'The Fiat Dino is a car which is sheer enchantment for the enthusiast to handle. Small enough to be driven fast on narrow roads, it is also sufficiently large to be very comfortable... Unlike any previous sports car of advanced racing design, the Dino will have the worldwide service organization of Fiat behind it, so it can be regarded as thoroughly practical transportation rather than a pampered status symbol'.

In *The Motor*, Charles Bulmer wrote: ' It is difficult to think of any sports car engine more enjoyable .... And if you didn't know the Dino had a live axle you would think it had very good independent suspension all round'.

The Fiat Dino spider, which made its debut in 1966 with a detuned version of the 2-litre engine used for the Ferrari Dino 206GT, owed its chunky but appealing styling to Pininfarina. It was Ferrari's desire to make a major impact in Formula 2 racing (which never really happened) and to have an engine suitable for a lower-priced road car (which did) which led to the collaboration with Fiat.

A hardtop version of the Dino spider was created but could scarcely be termed an aesthetic success.

The Dino spider was quickly followed by a four-seater coupe, the styling in this instance being by Bertone. This was a graceful looking car which offered ample passenger space.

Inevitably the Fiat Dinos became a popular base for experimentation by coachbuilders, in this case Pininfarina again, who produced this cross between a GT coupe and an estate.

Considerably more pleasing was Pininfarina's suggestion for a berlinetta based on the spider body shape, although it, too, never went into series production.

Despite all this enthusiasm, the Fiat Dino was not a car that made a great impact. The original 2-litre models were sold mainly in the Italian market. Production records show that 1,163 spiders and 3,670 coupes were made up to 1969 when, at around the time of the release of Ferrari's Dino 246, both Fiat Dinos were uprated to '2400'.

This involved the use of the cast-iron-block 2,419cc engine – making 180bhp in Fiat specification – and also brought independent rear suspension. Fiat favoured the use of iron for the engine block because it was cheaper and made for a quieter engine. Contrary to popular belief at the time, the 2.4-litre Dino block was not shared with the simpler, two-cam V6 of the new 130 saloon and coupe; that was a completely different engine with cylinders disposed at 60 rather than 65 degrees.

The new rear suspension, however, was shared with the 130 – a semi-trailing-arm system with strut-type dampers and separate coil springs. Also shared was the ZF five-speed gearbox, replacing the original Dino transmission which derived from the 2300. Like the Dino 246GT, the Fiats adopted five-stud wheels. Otherwise, outwardly they were little changed.

The Dino 2400 was exported, though rather half-heartedly. Some came to Britain, though like the 2-litre version, it was never made in right-hand-drive form.

It was a much improved car, but it didn't last long. By the end of 1972, the Fiat Dino had faded away, with 420 spider and 2,398 coupe 2400s produced. It had done its job for Ferrari, and Fiat had by then taken Maranello under its corporate wing. Indeed, the Ferrari factory had been called upon to make the Fiat Dino alongside its pure-bred cousin in the last period of its production. Though the Fiats were significantly cheaper than the Ferrari version, there seemed little point in continuing with both. Fiat concentrated on the prestige 131 coupe for their own range – and on building up the production of real Ferraris, even if most of them still carried the Dino name.

Just as the Ferrari Dino 206GT gave way to the 246GT, so were the Fiat Dinos uprated into 2.4-litre cars. Note the different grille design on this spider 2400, which was announced at the end of 1969. The change of engine was accompanied by a switch to independent rear suspension.

The changes to the Bertone-bodied coupe were more extensive and included a new grille, much more sumptuous upholstery as part of a complete interior redesign, and again the introduction of independent rear suspension.

CHAPTER 12

The wider family

Dino-engined Lancias

Lancia-Ferraris date back to the 1950s, when the innovative Lancia D50 V8 Formula 1 cars were handed over to Ferrari by the retiring and financially troubled Lancia team. In October 1969, less than five months after Enzo Ferrari and Gianni Agnelli had made their agreement, Lancia also fell into the arms of Fiat. Potentially, all kinds of cross-fertilization became possible...

The first example came about in a surprising way. The Bertone styling house shook everyone at the 1970 Turin Show when they exhibited an incredible wedge-shaped coupe powered by a centrally-mounted Lancia Fulvia engine and transmission. They called it the Stratos. After the cries of 'impractical!' had evaporated, Lancia appreciated that within this radical (and, frankly, unusable) show-stopper was the germ of an idea.

Their Fulvia 1600HF rally car was becoming uncompetitive in the face of lightweight rear-engined Alpine-Renaults. A purpose-built rally car, made in sufficient numbers to qualify for Group 4 homologation, seemed the only available route. What that ultra-low Stratos had demonstrated was a very compact mid-engined coupe. Now, if it were to be made taller and have more power, such a car could be just what they needed. More power could come from a Dino engine.

The 'proper' Stratos HF from Bertone appeared a year later with a 190bhp Ferrari V6 and Dino transmission amidships. It had two conventional doors at the side instead of the original's single opening in the nose, was 10in higher and had a tight 86in wheelbase. It was 19in shorter overall than the similarly-powered Dino 246GT.

It was designed around a strong sheet-steel monocoque forming the cockpit, on to which subframes were mounted.

Everything was designed to take up the minimum space, but still be easy to maintain and replace. Strut-type suspension was used at the rear, with a reversed lower wishbone and long radius rod, and there were double wishbones at the front.

The Stratos made its rally debut on the 1972 Tour de Corse and scored its first win in the 1973 Firestone Rally, in Spain. It came close to winning the Targa Florio that year, eventually finishing second in the last of this classic series to qualify as a World Championship sports car race.

It had been hoped to build the necessary 500 cars for homologation by March 1974, but it did not gain the necessary certification until October that year; even then, it is a moot point whether the requisite 500 were actually produced...

It was the start of a long and illustrious rally career. The Stratos was perfectly specified for most of the rallies of the time, on tarmac or loose surfaces. It was to make Lancia World Rally Champions three years in a row (1974, 1975 and 1976) and was still winning in 1978 when Markku Alen used a Group 5 version in the last official works entry for a Stratos in the Giro d'Italia.

A year later, an inspired drive by Bernard Darniche in a privately-entered Stratos gave the model its fourth Monte Carlo Rally victory. In seven years the Stratos had scored 82 international wins, 14 of them in World Rally Championship events.

During the 'prototype' phase (before homologation), Lancia had experimented with 24-valve heads and turbocharging to increase the Stratos' power. The 270bhp 24-valve engine became standard competition wear as the car's career went on, and the Group 5 turbo version was planned for a serious attempt on sports car racing in 1975 and 1976. This long-tailed car, with a

113

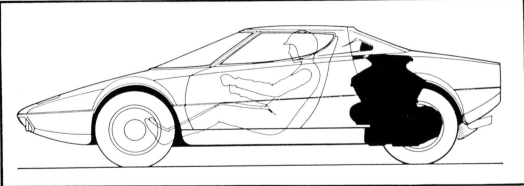

Even by show car standards, the wedge-shaped projectile which Bertone produced for the 1970 Turin Show under the name Lancia Stratos was something of a sensation. But although utterly impractical in the form presented, it provided Lancia with a germ of an idea for a replacement for their Fulvia 1600HF rally car. Bertone was asked to return to the drawingboard, and the result, a year later, was a very different outline and a Stratos which was to take the rally world by storm.

single turbocharger on a 12-valve engine, developed 480bhp in racing trim and as much as 570bhp with higher boost. By comparison with the rally cars, it was not successful, though it did win the 1976 Giro d'Italia.

After the Stratos, the Fiat Group's competition activities (aside from Ferrari) concentrated on the Fiat 131 Abarth for rallying and a Group 5 version of the Lancia Monte Carlo for endurance racing. Lancia and Ferrari were not to work together again until the Lancia LC2 endurance racer of 1983. This was the most serious competition application for the V8 Dino engine and used a version designated 268C of 2,593cc, with twin KKK turbochargers, developing 560bhp at 8,500rpm and up to 800bhp in 'qualifying' trim. Fast but unreliable, the LC2 had three seasons, showing no more than flashes of brilliance, before the team withdrew, leaving the World Sports Car Championship to Porsche and Jaguar.

The Ferrari involvement in the Stratos and the LC2 was simply as a convenient 'in house' supplier of power units. These Lancias carried no Ferrari badging and there was not even a prancing horse sticker among the line-up of trade sponsors' decals on the sills of the LC2. Fiat management, however, cherished an idea of a flagship car which incorporated Ferrari

Prototype of the Stratos HF, a smoothly contoured coupe powered by the Ferrari Dino 246GT's V6 engine, which again was mounted transversely amidships. The car would undergo many detail changes before it finally went into series production in 1974.

The addition of necessary wings and body skirts has done much to spoil the silhouette of this turbocharged Stratos, which was raced under Group 5 regulations by Carlo Facetti and Vittorio Brambilla but with only limited success.

The Lancia LC2 produced for endurance racing in 1983 was powered by a 2.6-litre version of the Dino V8 engine, the output of which was boosted with the aid of twin KKK turbochargers.

The Lancia Thema 8.32 has to be one of the most discreet-looking 150mph saloons of all time. Its designation refers to the number of cylinders and the number of valves in its Ferrari Dino 3-litre engine; this drives the front wheels, although a four-wheel-drive version of the car is planned for the future.

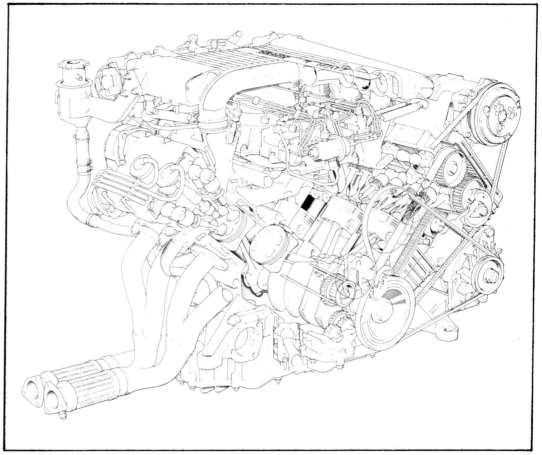

A superbly executed cutaway drawing of the Ferrari Dino QV engine as fitted to the Lancia Thema 8.32. The use of 90-degree rather than 180-degree crank throws contributes to a level of flexibility appropriate for a prestige saloon.

technology and was proud to admit it.

The Lancia Thema 8.32, announced in April 1986, is known within the company as 'Ghidella's baby'. The chief of Fiat Auto, Vittorio Ghidella, saw this as the perfect amalgam – a Ferrari engine in a four-door saloon of the kind that Maranello would never offer. It would give a prestige lift to the Lancia marque.

The designation 8.32 says eight cylinders and 32 valves, so this is the *Quattrovalvole* V8 engine with Bosch KE3 Jetronic fuel injection. The size chosen is the 308QV's 2,927cc. Mounted transversely, of course, but with an important difference – this is the first time that Ferrari has been called upon to drive the front wheels.

The Thema 8.32 is the most powerful front-wheel-drive car on the European market. In this F105L form, the Ferrari V8

Yet another use has been found for the Ferrari V8 engine in this Alba-Ferrari with which Martino Finotto, Carlo Facetti and Rugero Melgrati contested the Camel Light class of the 1988 IMSA GT Championship in the United States.

produces 215bhp at 6,750rpm. It differs from the 308QV engine in several respects, notably the use of a crankshaft with 90-degree throws instead of 180 degrees. The aim was to make a smoother, more flexible engine, better suited to a prestige saloon.

The result is a spacious luxury car of terrific performance – 149mph maximum speed and 0-100km/h (62mph) in less than 7sec. Though Lancia engineers admit that, longer term, they will fit four-wheel drive, thanks to careful suspension development the front-drive 8.32 is remarkably well behaved. It doesn't feel – or sound – quite like a Ferrari, but it is an impressive machine for which, not surprisingly, demand has far exceeded supply.

A special assembly line for the 8.32 was established at Lancia's old S. Paulo plant in Turin. Production there is limited to about 2,000 cars a year by the supply of engines from Maranello.

Though the five-spoke 'star' wheels have a Ferrari look about them, there is no sign of the identity of the engine manufacturer. Why? The official line is that they wanted to keep this flagship model low-key, discreet. It is said, though, than Enzo Ferrari himself vetoed the use of his name on the outside of the car. Open the bonnet, and the 8.32 shows its heart. Cast lettering on the engine's elaborately shaped inlet manifold proudly proclaims 'Lancia by Ferrari'.

CHAPTER 13

Made in Maranello

What goes into a Ferrari

Maranello, a village not far from Modena in the Po basin, the centre of northern Italy, enjoys a fame beyond its size, thanks to the presence of Ferrari. Some 1,300 people work within the cluster of low buildings on the outskirts of the village. There, they build supercars.

Another 216 are employed at the racing department, based alongside the test track in nearby Fiorano, and there are 266 people at Scaglietti, the company's body-making facility in Modena.

Ferrari made 3,942 cars in 1987. That was a record, but the total since the company started making cars for sale in 1947 is only about 45,000 – or rather less than the annual output of Porsche or Jaguar.

The ratio of cars built to number of employees – an important index of efficiency in the volume car business – does not apply here. Ferraris are not ordinary and neither is the way they are put together. Even now, following Fiat's major investment in new equipment over the last few years, the craftsman rather than the button-pusher plays the major role in the making of a Ferrari.

Power units are assembled by skilled fitters, working in small teams, who know every millimetre of Ferrari engines. It is painstaking work, requiring care and concentration. Each completed engine has four hours of testing on a dynamometer before being released to the car assembly lines.

There are two parallel U-shaped lines, for eight-cylinder (GTB, GTS and Mondial) and 12-cylinder (Testarossa and 412) models. Here too, the work is thorough and the cars are pushed from one station to the next only when the fitters are happy that their part of the operation has been completed satisfactorily.

To one side of the factory are craftsmen (and women) of a different kind. This is the trim area, where British-sourced Connolly hides are shaped and stitched to provide Ferraris' distinctive leather interiors.

It is all a very long way from the robotized and automatically-guided car production elsewhere in the Fiat empire. But where high technology can benefit small-volume production, Ferrari has it.

Most significant are the Green Giants – 15 massive Mandelli computer-controlled boring and milling machines that take over where hand-set lathes and jigs left off. They can carry out 23 processes and 110 operations and do so with accuracy and repeatability that even the most skilled operator can't match with the old machines.

Some 70% of a Ferrari is made by Ferrari. They are unusual among specialist car makers in having their own foundry, in a separate building across the yard from the assembly area, producing aluminium alloy castings which will be machined by the Green Giants.

There, two large gas-fired ovens prepare high-silicon aluminium. The molten alloy is ladled into individual moulds – permanent ones for intricate cylinder head castings and the sand type for the many others.

Around the factory, the neat stacks of these automotive sculptures – V8 and V12 blocks, cylinder heads, gearbox casings – are an engineer's delight.

Of course, many raw components are brought in from outside suppliers. Crankshaft forgings, for example, come from Teksid, a Fiat subsidiary, while some camshafts are supplied by Alfa

119

Romeo, now also an associate company through Fiat.

Indeed, the skeleton of a 328 or Mondial – its tubular space-frame chassis – is also sourced elesewhere. In this case, the supplier is Vaccari, of Modena, conveniently close to Scaglietti where the bodies take shape. The main body panels, steel and aluminium, are pressed at ITCA, another Fiat division, located near Turin.

Scaglietti build the bodies on to the chassis, using a jig system and hand-operated welding equipment. There are two lines there, one for the GTB/GTS and the other for the Mondial (Testarossa and 412 bodies are made at Pininfarina, in Turin). Though the pressing is done elsewhere, the folding and trimming of flanges and soldering of body seams still requires skilful handwork.

Incongruously, Scaglietti also make tractor cabs for Fiat; a legacy of more difficult times when Ferrari could only justify

Drilling a crankshaft in the days of Dino 246 production at Maranello. Today, much of the boring and milling work is done by computer-controlled machinery.

An impressive quantity of pre-machined V8 block castings awaiting transfer from Ferrari's own foundry to the machine shop on the other side of the factory yard.

A Ferrari V8 engine close to completion. During the build process engines are mounted on trolleys, which can be raised to a convenient working height by being placed over a ram-operated lift built into the floor.

Trolley-mounted 328 transmissions ready for transporting into the final assembly area. Approximately 4,000 units are required annually.

investment in new plant if they could share its capacity.

The complete but unpainted bodies – and the cabs – make the 10-mile journey to Maranello by truck. At one time, Ferrari paint finish was a justifiable area of criticism. Today, finish and paint durability are much better, thanks to the new paint plant. Commissioned in 1980, it is a sophisticated facility for a car producer of Ferrari's size.

The first process is to immerse the bodies in a cataphoretic primer tank. Robot sprayers then apply a primer colour coat – mostly pink, for red cars (which account for some 70% of orders) but otherwise grey. But the nine top coats are applied by hand, and other components from bumpers to small finisher panels are also all sprayed by hand. There is close attention to the quality of finish at each stage.

But glance at the cars on the assembly lines and something looks wrong. Most are red, but they are shiny and uneven, like a piece of cheese on a supermarket shelf. In fact, just like it, for

A Mondial in the making. Body panels are pressed at a division of Fiat near Turin, then transported to Scaglietti in Modena for welding to the locally built spaceframe chassis, the completed structure then being taken by truck to Maranello for painting and finishing on the Ferrari premises.

after trying all sorts of different ways of protecting the paintwork during the car's progress through the factory, Ferrari now cover them with thin polythene sheet.

Assembly takes place at a steady, unhurried rate. Suspension sub-assemblies wait beside the lines and, where appropriate, are mounted to engine and transmission units before the whole is offered up to the body/chassis on the overhead line by hydraulic lift.

The cling film is removed only when all the end-of-the-line tests are completed. Those include a 200km road test and, for some, a workout at the Fiorano track. Then it is back to the inspection area, where any mechanical defects are rectified, the car is cleaned, and then thoroughly examined for paint and finish imperfections.

Twelve or 13 eight-cylinder cars come out of the factory every working day (and four or five 12-cylinder models). It takes about two months for an individual car to pass from the start of production to being ready for delivery.

Maranello is working very close to maximum capacity these days. Though they sanctioned some £30 million of expenditure on production facilities between 1984 and 1986, and anticipate investing some 15% of Ferrari's turnover in new technology in the future, the idea of the Fiat bosses is not to make many more cars per year. They have set a ceiling of around 4,000 annual production, regardless of how strong the demand is around the world.

What is planned is the wider application of Ferrari's technical expertise through an offshoot called Ferrari Engineering. Its aim is the kind of contract work for which Porsche and Lotus are renowned. Associate companies within Fiat, including Lancia and Alfa Romeo, may benefit – and so will other organizations outside the automotive industry.

Unlike Porsche and Lotus, they will not sell their services to other car companies. Fiat can't take the risk of devaluing Ferrari. As one of their senior executives explained: 'Ferrari is a precious object, a rare thing. We want to keep it that way.'

A stack of left-hand-drive 328GTB and GTS facias with intrument panels already installed ready for use in the assembly area.

The V8 assembly line at Maranello with a 328GTB leading the way. The front compartment lid is one of the last items to be fitted.

Protective cling film is applied to Ferraris before they leave the assembly area and is only removed after all the checks have been completed.

The test and finishing area is the final call for this 328GTB before despatch from the factory. Nine coats of paint have been applied by hand-held guns in the spray shop, but this is where the final gloss is produced.

APPENDIX A

Technical specifications

Dino 206GT–produced 1967 to 1969
Construction: Light-alloy panelling over tubular frame.
Engine: 65-deg V6-cyl, 4ohc, 86 × 57mm, 1,986cc, CR 9.2:1, 4-bearing crankshaft, 3 twin-choke Weber 40DCN carbs. Maximum power 180bhp at 8,000rpm; maximum torque 138lb/ft at 6,500rpm.
Transmission: Mechanically-operated single-dry-plate clutch. 5-speed all-synchromesh gearbox and limited-slip differential. Final-drive ratio 3.423:1 (17/58). Gearbox ratios 4.424, 2.588, 1.897, 1.488, 1.132, reverse 3.267:1. (Later cars with transmission ratios as 246GT below.)
Running gear: Ifs, upper and lower wishbones, coil springs, telescopic dampers and anti-roll bar; irs, upper and lower wishbones, coil springs, telescopic dampers and anti-roll bar. Servo-assisted hydraulic brakes with ventilated discs on all wheels. Rack-and-pinion steering. Cast-alloy wheels with 185 HR14 tyres.
Dimensions: Wheelbase 7ft 5.7in; front track 4ft 6in; rear track 4ft 5in; length 13ft 6in; width 5ft 7in; height 3ft 6in. Turning circle 37ft. Kerb weight 2,173lb.

Dino 246GT–produced 1969 to 1974
Construction: Steel panelling over tubular frame.
Engine: 65-deg V6-cyl, 4ohc, 92.5 × 60mm, 2,418cc, CR 9:1, 4-bearing crankshaft, 3 twin-choke Weber 40DCF carbs. Maximum power 195bhp at 7,600rpm; maximum torque 165lb/ft at 5,500rpm. USA spec: 175bhp at 7,000rpm; 160lb/ft at 5,000rpm.
Transmission: Mechanically-operated single-dry-plate clutch. 5-speed all-synchromesh gearbox and limited-slip differential. Final-drive ratio 3.625:1 (16/58). Gearbox ratios 3.76, 2.59, 1.863, 1.376, 1.046, reverse 3.255:1.
Running gear: As Dino 206GT except 205/70 VR14 tyres.
Dimensions: Wheelbase 7ft 8in; front track 4ft 7in; rear track 4ft 8in; length 13ft 11in; width 5ft 7in; height 3ft 9in. Turning circle 37ft. Kerb weight 2,609lb.

Dino 246GTS–produced 1972 to 1974
As for Dino 246GT except kerb weight 2,585lb.

308GT4–produced 1974 to 1980
Construction: Steel panelling over tubular frame.
Engine: 90-deg V8-cyl, 4ohc, 81 × 71mm, 2,926cc, CR 8.8:1, 5-bearing crankshaft, 4 twin-choke Weber 40DCNF carbs. Maximum power 250bhp at 7,700rpm; maximum torque 210lb/ft at 5,000 rpm. USA spec: 240bhp at 6,600rpm; 181lb/ft at 5,000rpm.
Transmission: Single-dry-plate clutch with cushioned centre plate. 5-speed all-synchromesh gearbox and limited-slip differential. Final-drive ratio 3.5:1 (18/63), later cars 3.71:1 (17/63). Gearbox ratios 3.23, 2.235, 1.619, 1.2, 0.897, reverse 3:1. Later cars 3.418, 2.353, 1.693, 1.244, 0.952, reverse 3.247:1.
Running gear: Ifs, upper and lower wishbones, coil springs, telescopic dampers and anti-roll bar; irs, upper and lower wishbones, coil springs, telescopic dampers and anti-roll bar. Servo-assisted hydraulic brakes with ventilated discs on all wheels. Rack-and-pinion steering. Cast-alloy wheels with 205/70 VR14 tyres. Reduced-section 'get you home' spare.
Dimensions: Wheelbase 8ft 4.4in; front track 4ft 9.5in; rear track 4ft 9.5in; length 14ft 1.3in; width 5ft 11in; height 3ft 10.5in. Turning circle 41ft. Kerb weight 2,866lb.

208GT4–produced 1975 to 1980
As for 308GT4 except engine 90-deg V8-cyl, 4ohc, 66.8 × 71mm, 1,991cc, CR 9:1, 5-bearing crankshaft, 4 twin-choke Weber 34DCNF carbs. Maximum power 170bhp at 7,700rpm; maximum torque 137lb/ft at 4,900rpm. Final-drive ratio 4.6:1 (15/69). 5th gear ratio 0.877:1. 195/70 VR14 tyres.

308GTB–produced 1975 to 1980
Construction: Glass-reinforced plastic (early cars) then steel panelling over tubular frame.
Engine: 90-deg V8-cyl, 4ohc, 81 × 71mm, 2,926cc, CR 8.8:1, 5-bearing crankshaft, 4 twin-choke Weber 40DCNF carbs. Maximum power 250bhp at 7,700rpm; maximum torque 210lb/ft at 5,000rpm. USA spec: 230bhp at 7,700rpm; 209lb/ft at 5,000rpm.

Transmission: Single-dry-plate clutch with cushioned centre plate. 5-speed all-synchromesh gearbox and limited-slip differential. Final-drive ratio 3.71:1 (17/63). Gearbox ratios 3.418, 2.353, 1.693, 1.244, 0.925, reverse 3.247:1.
Running gear: Ifs, upper and lower wishbones, coil springs, telescopic dampers and anti-roll bar; irs, upper and lower wishbones, coil springs, telescopic dampers and anti-roll bar. Servo-assisted hydraulic brakes with ventilated discs on all wheels. Rack-and-pinion steering. Cast-alloy wheels with 205/70 VR14 tyres. Reduced-section 'get you home' spare.
Dimensions: Wheelbase 7ft 8.1in; front track 4ft 9.9in; rear track 4ft 9.9in; length 14ft 6.2in; width 5ft 7.7in; height 3ft 8.1in. Turning circle 39.3ft. Kerb weight 2,784lb.

308GTS–produced 1977 to 1980
As for 308GTB except kerb weight 2,859lb.

308GTBi–produced 1981 to 1982
As for 308GTB except maximum power 214bhp at 6,600rpm; maximum torque 179lb/ft at 4,600rpm. USA spec: 205bhp at 6,600rpm; 180lb/ft at 5,000rpm.

308GTSi–produced 1981 to 1982
As for 308GTS except maximum power and torque as 308GTBi.

308GTBi Quattrovalvole–produced 1982 to 1985
As for 308GTB/GTBi except 9.2:1, Bosch K-Jetronic mechanical fuel injection. Maximum power 240bhp at 7,000rpm; maximum torque 192lb/ft at 5,000rpm. USA spec: CR 8.6:1. 230bhp at 6,800rpm; 188lb/ft at 5,500rpm. Tyre size 220/55 VR390.
Dimensions: Wheelbase 7ft 8.5in; front track 4ft 9.5in; width 5ft 8.1in; height 3ft 8.4in. Kerb weight 2,784lb.

308GTSi Quattrovalvole–produced 1982 to 1985
As for 308GTBi Quattrovalvole except kerb weight 2,859lb.

208 Turbo–produced from 1982
As for 308GTBi except engine dimensions as 208GT4. CR 7:1, KKK turbocharger running at maximum of 8.5psi (0.6bar) boost pressure, Bosch K-Jetronic fuel injection. Maximum power 220bhp at 7,000rpm; maximum torque 174lb/ft at 4,800rpm. Final-drive ratio 4.313:1 (16/69). Gearbox ratios 3.59; 2.353, 1.693, 1.244, 0.881, reverse 3.247:1.

328GTB–produced from 1985
As for 308GTB except engine 83 × 73mm, 3,185cc, CR 9.8:1. Maximum power 270bhp at 7,000rpm; maximum torque 224lb/ft at 5,500rpm. Kerb weight 2,784lb.

328GTS–produced from 1985
As for 328GTB except kerb weight 2,806lb.

Mondial 8–produced 1980 to 1982
Construction: Steel panelling over tubular frame. Rear engine cover and front bonnet manufactured from aluminium alloy.
Engine and transmission as 308GTBi.
Running gear as 308GTBi except 240/55 VR390 tyres.
Dimensions: Wheelbase 8ft 8.3in; front track 4ft 10.9in; rear track 4ft 11.7in; length 15ft 0.3in; width 5ft 10.5in; height 4ft 1.6in. Turning circle 39.4ft. Kerb weight 3,108lb.

Mondial Quattrovalvole–produced 1982 to 1985
Construction as Mondial 8.
Engine and transmission as 308GTBi QV.
Running gear as Mondial 8 except 220/55 VR390 tyres front, 240/55 VR390 tyres rear. Kerb weight 3,152lb.

Mondial Cabriolet Quattrovalvole–produced 1984 to 1985
As Mondial Quattrovalvole except kerb weight 3,086lb.

3.2 Mondial–produced from 1985
As Mondial Quattrovalvole except engine as 328GTB.

3.2 Mondial Cabriolet–produced from 1985
As 3.2 Mondial except kerb weight 3,086lb.

288GTO–produced 1984 to 1985
Construction: Glass-fibre panelling over tubular frame with carbon-fibre bulkhead separating engine and cockpit.
Engine: 90-deg V8-cyl, 4ohc, 80 × 71mm, 2,855cc, CR 7.6:1, 5-bearing crankshaft, twin IHI turbochargers running at maximum of 11.3psi (0.8bar) boost pressure, Weber-Marelli electronic injection/ignition system. Maximum power 400bhp at 7,000rpm; maximum torque 366lb/ft at 3,800rpm.
Transmission: Twin-plate clutch. 5-speed all-synchromesh gearbox mounted longitudinally and limited-slip differential. Final-drive ratio 2.9:1 (10/29). Gearbox ratios 3.692, 2.296, 1.636, 1.284, 1.022, reverse 3.282:1.
Running gear: Ifs, upper and lower wishbones, coil springs, telescopic dampers and anti-roll bar; irs, upper and lower wishbones, coil springs, telescopic dampers and anti-roll bar. Servo-assisted hydraulic brakes with ventilated discs on all wheels. Rack-and-pinion steering. Cast-alloy wheels with 225/55 VR16 tyres front, 265/50 VR16 tyres rear. Reduced-section get you home' spare.
Dimensions: Wheelbase 8ft 0.5in; front track 5ft 1.4in; rear track 5ft 1.4in; length 14ft 0.9in; width 6ft 3.2in; height 3ft 8.1in. Turning circle 39.4ft. Kerb weight 2,557lb.

F40–produced from 1987

Construction: Moulded carbon-fibre composite bodyshell integrated with tubular steel frame.
Engine: 90-deg V8 cyl, 4ohc, 81.9 × 69.5mm, 2,936cc, CR 7.8:1, 5-bearing crankshaft, twin IHI turbochargers running at maximum of 16psi (1.13bar) boost pressure, Weber-Marelli electronic injection/ignition system. Maximum power 478bhp at 7,800rpm; maximum torque 425lb/ft at 4,000rpm.
Transmission: Twin-plate clutch. 5-speed all-synchromesh gearbox mounted longitudinally and limited-slip differential. Alternative gearbox available with straight-cut gears.

Running gear: Ifs, upper and lower wishbones, coil springs, telescopic dampers and anti-roll bar; irs, upper and lower wishbones, coil springs, telescopic dampers and anti-roll bar. High-speed settings enable ride height to be reduced for optimum aerodynamics. Ventilated disc brakes on all wheels without servo-assistance. Cast-alloy wheels with 245/40 ZR17 tyres front, 335/35 ZR17 tyres rear.
Dimensions: Wheelbase 8ft 0.5in; front track 5ft 2.8in; rear track 5ft 3.4in; length 14ft 6.4in; width 6ft 6in; height 3ft 8.5in. Turning circle 39.4ft. Kerb weight 2,425lb.

APPENDIX B

Production figures and chassis numbers including UK market allocations

Models	Chassis numbers	Production	UK market
206GT	*00104GT-00402GT	150	5 (all LHD)
246GT series 1	00400GT-01116GT	357	
246GT series 2	01118GT-02130GT	507	488
246GT series 3	02132GT-08560GT	1,745	
246GTS	03408GT-08518GT	1,274	235
308GT4	07202GT-15604GT	2,826	547
308GTB	18677GT-34501GT	2,896	365
308GTS	22169GT-32101GT	3,219	184
308 GTBi	31327GT-42701GT	494	42
(incl. Mondial 8		703	74
308GTSi	31309GT-42703GT	1,743	67
308GTB QV		748	174
(incl. Mondial QV	43201GT-58301GT	1,149	216
and Cabriolet		628	24
288GTO	Not available	272	20 (all LHD)
328GTB			
328GTS	all current models		
3.2 Mondial			
3.2 Mondial Cabriolet			

Note: Owing to the nature of Ferrari's road car chassis numbering sequences, it has only been possible to indicate within which spread of chassis numbers the differing models fall. *Chassis number of prototype 206GT was 0840GT.

APPENDIX C

Performance figures

	Dino 246GT	Dino 308GT4	Dino 308GTB	Dino 308GTS	Mondial 8	Mondial 3.0QV	308GTBi QV	328GTB	328GTB	Mondial 3.2	Mondial 3.2	Mondial 3.2 Cabriolet	288 GTO
Mean max speed (mph)	148	154	154	150+	138	146.1	154.5	158.5	153	143	148.5	—	180
Acceleration (sec)													
0-30 mph	2.6	2.5	2.3	2.5	3.1	2.2	2.1	2.2	2.1	2.6	2.5	2.6	2.3
0-40 mph	3.6	3.6	3.3	3.4	4.6	3.3	3.0	3.0	—	3.8	3.4	—	—
0-50 mph	5.5	5.4	5.1	5.0	7.1	4.7	4.5	4.3	—	5.3	5.0	—	—
0-60 mph	7.1	6.9	6.5	6.6	9.3	6.4	5.7	5.5	5.5	6.8	6.3	7.0	5.0
0-70 mph	9.2	9.1	8.7	8.6	12.9	8.2	7.5	7.2	—	8.9	8.2	—	—
0-80 mph	11.4	11.4	10.8	10.6	16.0	10.2	9.2	8.9	—	10.8	10.0	11.7	7.7
0-90 mph	14.5	15.2	13.8	13.5	21.7	13.0	11.6	11.3	—	13.9	11.9	—	—
0-100 mph	17.6	18.1	17.0	16.6	27.8	16.2	14.3	13.8	14.2	16.5	15.8	17.2	11.0
0-110 mph	22.0	22.4	20.4	20.9	37.7	20.7	17.2	16.7	—	20.1	19.2	—	—
0-120 mph	28.5	30.3	25.0	27.3	—	—	20.5	—	—	25.5	23.9	—	—
Standing ½ mile (sec)	15.4	14.9	14.8	15.0	—	14.5	14.2	14.1	14.1	14.9	14.8	—	—
Top Gear accel (sec)													
20-40 mph	8.4	—	—	—	—	9.3	8.1	7.4	7.4	8.5	8.0	—	—
30-50 mph	7.8	8.4	9.5	9.0	13.1	8.5	7.4	7.0	6.9	7.8	7.6	—	—
40-60 mph	7.8	7.9	8.4	7.9	—	8.6	7.3	7.0	6.7	7.6	7.1	—	—
50-70 mph	7.2	7.6	7.8	7.5	11.8	8.6	7.2	7.0	6.8	8.1	7.2	—	—
60-80 mph	7.3	7.7	7.2	7.8	—	8.7	7.3	7.1	6.8	8.5	7.7	—	—
70-90 mph	8.2	8.0	7.7	8.3	—	9.3	7.4	7.2	6.9	9.0	8.3	—	—
80-100 mph	8.9	8.7	8.8	9.3	—	10.6	7.4	7.9	7.4	9.9	9.3	—	—
Overall fuel consumption (mpg Imp)	16.1	19.8	19.2	—	16.8	18.6	19.6	18.9	16.2	16.8	15.9	—	—
Typical fuel consumption (mpg Imp)	23.0	21.8	21.0	—	—	20.0	23.0	22.5	18.3	18.5	21.0	19.2	15.6
Kerb test weight (lbs)	3035	3290	3220	3415	3560	—	3280	3372	—	3647	3643	3695	2720
Original test published	*Motor* 7/71	*Autocar* 3/76	*Autocar* 10/76	*Motor* 8/78	*C and D* 11/81	*Motor* 10/82	*Motor* 10/83	*Motor* 6/86	*Autocar* 4/88	*Autocar* 6/86	*Motor* 5/88	*R & T* 7/87	*R & T* 7/87